AN OUTLINE OF SILOZI GRAMMAR

GEORGE FORTUNE

Series Editor: MUBANGA E. KASHOKI

Bookworld Publishers

First Published in 1977 by the Institute for African Studies (now the Institute of Economic and Social Research), University of Zambia in *Language in Zambia; Grammatical Sketches.*

This edition is published by Bookworld Publishers
PO Box 32581, Lusaka, Zambia.
2001

Copyright © Institute of Economic and Social Research 1977

All rights reserved. No part of this publication may be reproduced, stored in a retrieval system, or transmitted, in any form or by any means electronic, mechanical, photocopying, recording or otherwise, without the prior permission of the publisher.

ISBN 9982 24 1591

Typesetting by Fergan Limited, Lusaka, Zambia.

Printed by Printech Limited, Lusaka, Zambia.

FOREWORD

There has been a lack of up to date descriptive grammars of Zambian languages suitable for use, either as teaching or as learning aids, at all levels of the Zambian education system. This lack has been keenly felt by teachers and learners alike. Many of the grammars that are available could be said to be inadequate or inappropriate in several respects. The oldest ones were written at a time when Latin or European languages generally were considered to be the prototype of all grammars, and thus they tended to be patterned in their arrangement, description and the terminology employed on Latin-based grammatical rules. Others were written in a style and language which presented serious problems of comprehension even to teachers. In a good many cases, the actual examples cited were unnatural, forced or not in accord with accepted usage. At the present moment many of these works have long been out of print.

In order to put in the hands of the teachers and learners grammatical descriptions which reflected more nearly the structural facts of their language, during 1970-71, the Survey of Language Use and Language Teaching in Zambia attempted to provide comprehensible grammatical descriptions of the seven Zambian languages officially prescribed for use in education, broadcasting and literacy programmes. The authors who volunteered or were approached to write them were specifically instructed to employ a comprehensible style and to keep technical terminology to the absolute minimum. The general reader was clearly in mind. It is hoped that with the publishing now of the grammatical outlines of iciBemba, siLozi, ciNyanja and iciTonga the original intention of providing grammatical descriptions of appeal to a wide audience, both lay and professional, will have been achieved.

As originally conceived, seven grammatical sketches representing all the seven officially approved Zambian languages, plus sketches of Town Bemba and Town Tonga, were to have been published as Part One in a projected three-part volume of **Language in Zambia,** incorporating the findings of the Zambia Language Survey. In the event, it was found necessary in the interest of reducing bulk and cost to abandon the original plan and to arrange to publish the sketches separately. Indeed, publishing them separately has the advantage of making them available in a convenient, less bulky size suitable for both teacher and student handling.

The Institute for African Studies (now the Institute of Economic and Social Research), University of Zambia, published in 1977 **Language in Zambia: Grammatical Sketches,** Volume 1, containing grammatical sketches or outlines of iciBemba and kiKaonde by Michael Mann and JL Wright respectively, plus a sketch of the main characteristics of Town Bemba by Mubanga E Kashoki. The plan at the time was to publish subsequently two follow-up volumes: first, Volume 2, to contain sketches of siLozi and Lunda and Luvale and second, Volume 3, to contain sketches of ciNyanja and iciTonga. In the event this plan was not adhered to. Only one volume was published in accordance with the original plan and this has been out of print for some time now.

It is in part for these reasons that it has been considered necessary to attend to the unfinished business initiated some two decades ago. Also, and more pertinently, the need for pedagogical and reference grammars of Zambian languages continues to be keenly felt. The matter has now been made more urgent following the recent (1996) decision of the Zambian Government to revert to the earlier policy of using local (i.e. Zambian) languages plus English as a media of instruction. As now re-arranged, in order to achieve what is felt to be a more logical arrangement, four grammatical sketches of iciBemba, siLozi, ciNyanja and iciTonga will be published separately beginning with the first volume containing a grammatical outline of iciBemba.

Co-sponsored by the Institute for African Studies, (the present Institute of Economic and Social Research University of Zambia), the main volume **Language in Zambia,** was published in 1978 by the International African Institute (IAI) partly subsidised by funds from the Ford Foundation. The Institute gratefully acknowledges the permission granted by the Foundation, the sponsors of the language survey of which the material published herein is a partial outcome, to have the sketches published separately. Gratitude is also due to the authors of the sketches for their contribution in a field in which much remains to be done.

Other acknowledgements are due to Bookworld Publishers for publishing the sketches in collaboration with the Institute; to the editors of **Language in Zambia,** Sirarpi Ohannesssian and Mubanga E Kashoki, for carrying out the bulk of the necessary initial editorial work; to Dr. Tom Gorman who was detailed to bring a general stylistic consistency to the sketches; and to the secretarial Institute staff for preparing the typescript. Above all, the eventual publication of the sketches owes much to the Zambian Government, in particular the Ministry of Education, and to the University of Zambia for their interest and support and for providing a conducive environment in which fruitful research work could take place during the life of the Survey of Language Use Language Teaching in Zambia.

Mubanga E Kashoki
Professor of African Languages
INSTITUTE OF ECONOMIC AND SOCIAL RESEARCH
UNIVERSITY OF ZAMBIA
EDITOR

INTRODUCTION

The home of siLozi is the Western Province of Zambia, but it is far from being the only language spoken there. There are three groups of languages spoken in the province of much longer standing than siLozi, namely Luyana, Tonga and Nkoya. These groups of languages are spoken in the east-central and west, in the southwest and south, and in the northeast of the province respectively. SiLozi is the language of the central plain. Originally a form of Southern Sotho, it was brought into the country by the Kololo conquerors who, under their chief, Sebitwane, overcame the Luyi in 1840. As a Sotho language it may have been somewhat modified by the time the invaders reached the Zambezi owing to their wanderings and their contacts with the peoples on their way whom they met or absorbed. The Kololo were the dominant tribe in what is now the Western Province for three successive reigns, those of their chiefs Sebitwane, Sekeletu and Mbololo, but in 1864, Sipopa, a descendant of the old Luyi chiefs, re-established himself in power on the Barotse flood plain.

In the restoration, most of the Kololo men were killed. They had already been much reduced in number by fever and civil strife. The women and children became the property of the Luyi chiefs, and it must have been due to their influence, and that of the administrative changes of the preceding twenty-five years, that the language of the Kololo survived under the name of siLozi. Though much influenced by Luyana, it is still correctly classified as a language of the Sotho group and is understood in neighbouring Botswana.

SiLozi is spoken almost exclusively in the central Barotse plain to the north and south of Mongu, and on either side of the Zambezi to a considerable distance inland. It is also spoken along the river, in varying degrees, all the way to Livingstone, where it is the main African language in use. In addition, siLozi is spoken as a lingua franca all over the Western province and is the language of administration, education and general communication where English is not used. In the 1990 Census of Population, Housing and Agriculture the Lozi-speaking population was enumerated under the "Barotse Group" (which included the Nyengo, Lozi, Subiya, Nkoya and others). The group totalled 527,410, of which 447,852 constituted the number of speakers termed "Lozi" in the census. As a lingua franca, siLozi was placed in fourth position behind iciBemba, ciNyanja and iciTonga in the 1980 Census of Population and Housing. A decade later, the 1990 Census of Population showed the situation as remaining largely unchanged, once again siLozi coming in fourth place, the applicable statistics being 29.9 percent (iciBemba), 11 percent (iciTonga), 7.8 percent (ciNyanja) and 6.4 percent (siLozi). Overall, to be regarded as of the greatest relevance is the fact that within Zambia siLozi at present is counted among the five major languages, along with English, iciBemba, ciNyanja and iciTonga, which are spoken predominantly by the national population.

UNITS OF SOUND AND UNITS OF GRAMMAR

Spoken languages, like coins, have a twofold aspect and may be regarded, analysed and described from either side. They have a *phonological* aspect and a *morphological* aspect. From the phonological aspect we find that siLozi has a certain inventory of sound units which are combined in certain regular and recurrent ways. The term used for these units of sound is the *phoneme*.

From the morphological aspect we find that siLozi is also a structure of grammatical units which are also combined in certain ways. The term used for these grammatical units is the *morpheme*.

Under the heading *PHONOLOGY* we shall give a very condensed account of the phonemes of siLozi and of their combinations into the larger unit of the syllable. Under the heading *MORPHOLOGY* we shall give a somewhat more extended, but still very condensed, account of the classes of morpheme in siLozi and the way they combine into larger units which we shall call *grammatical constructions*.

ACKNOWLEDGEMENTS

In writing this "Outline" I have relied heavily on the works cited in the Bibliography, particularly on the two morphological studies by Mr., now Dr., D.F. Gowlett. The examples cited have been checked with Mr. R. Sitali, a siLozi-speaking informant whose help has been invaluable. The method of presentation follows the constituent structure model of analysis and description. The treatment of the phonology is deficient in that tone and length of vowels have not been adequately treated. Long and geminate vowels are spelt in the same way by duplication of the same letter, but length has been indicated only in the relative prefixes. The current orthography marks neither length nor tone. In Mr. D.F. Gowlett's articles, *A Selection of Lozi Folktales and Riddles, African Studies,* 30, Nos. 1 and 2, long vowels were marked with a macron. Finally I am grateful to Professor Mubanga E. Kashoki for additions to this Introduction which bring it up to date.

PHONOLOGY

Syllables in siLozi normally consist of a **consonant,** or a **consonant cluster,** followed by a **vowel.** Less commonly, syllables may consist of a vowel alone, or of a **nasal consonant** alone. These three types of syllable may be symbolised as follows:

(i) Consonant + vowel   CV
    Consonant cluster + vowel   CCV
(ii) Vowel alone   V
(iii) Nasal alone (only at the beginning or end of a word)   N

Each syllable carries a unit of tone and length, normally by means of its nuclear vowel. Syllabic nasal consonants, being resonants like vowels, may carry tone and length in the absence of a nuclear vowel,

e.g.   *mu-tu*   (person)   (1)[1]   is syllabically   CV-CV
       u-fi?   (which one?)   (1)   ”   ”   V-CV
       m-me   (mother)   (1a)   ”   ”   N-CV

VOWELS

There are five vowel phonemes in siLozi. Two are **high,** one being articulated with the front of the tongue high up in the front of the mouth, and the other with the back of the tongue high up at the back of the mouth. The first is pronounced, with spread lips and the second with rounded lips. These two vowels are spelt /i/ and /u/.

---

[1] A number in brackets after a word refers to the class of that noun. Noun classes are discussed on pages 11-20.

Two other vowels are of **medium** height, being articulated in the front and at the back of the mouth, and again with spread and rounded lips respectively. These vowels are spelt /e/ and /o/.

The fifth vowel is articulated with the tongue in a **low** and central position, and with the lips held neutrally between a spread and rounded, position. This vowel is spelt /a/.

e.g. mina   (you - plural)
      luna   (we)
      wena   (you)
      wona   (it)   (3)

CONSONANTS

The consonant phonemes of siLozi are listed in the following table. Their manner and place of articulation are indicated by the terms of the horizontal and vertical columns respectively.

		Labial	Alveolar	Palatal	Velar Glottal
Stops	- Voiceless	p	t	c	k
	- Voiced	b	d	j	g
Spirants	- Voiceless	f	s	sh	h
	- Voiced		z		
Approximants	- Voiced	w	l	y	
Nasals	- Voiced	m	n	ny	ŋ

The symbols used for the phonemes in the chart are also those employed in the standard spelling of siLozi today save that /ŋ/, when it occurs as a syllabic margin, is spelt ñ. In this study the letter (ŋ) will be used in order to spell the phoneme /ŋ/ when it is a single syllabic margin,

e.g.   teŋi   (there)

or when it clusters with /w/,

e.g.   ŋŋwi   (one)   (9)

When /ŋ/ occurs before the velar stops /k/ or /g/, it will be spelt as in the standard spelling, that is as (nk) and (ng),

e.g.   miongu (phonemically, /mioŋgu/)   (pumpkins)   (4)

The phoneme /ny/ is also spelt (n) when it comes before the palatal stops /c/ or /j/, that is, as (nc) and (nj).

The following consonant clusters combine with vowels to form syllables:

(a)	nasals + stops	:	/mp, nt, nc, nk, mb, nd, nj, ng/
(b)	nasals + spirants	:	/ns, nz/
(c)	stops + /w/	:	/pw, tw, cw, kw, bw/
(d)	spirants + /w/	:	/fw, sw, shw, hw, zw/
(e)	nasals + /w/	:	/mw, nw, nyw, ŋw/
(f)	nasals + stops + /w/	:	/mpw, ntw, ncw, nkw, mbw, ndw, njw, ngw/
(g)	nasals + spirants + /w/	:	/nsw, nzw/
(h)	labials + /y/	:	/py, by, my, mpy, mby/
(i)	alveolar approximant + /y/:		/ly/

TONE AND LENGTH

Syllables, which are otherwise identical in regard to their consonants and vowels, may differ in two other different but related ways. They may differ in tone, one being high, indicated as H, and the other low, indicated as L. They may also differ in length, one being long and the other short. Syllables may be either short or long. Short syllables carry only one tone which is either high (marked (´)) or low (marked (`)),

e.g. *mù-tù*   (person)   (1)
      mù-tú ù-fi?   (which person?) (1)

Long syllables carry a sequence of two tones which may be either both high, both low, or high-low. These sequences may be symbolised as HH, LL and HL. Syllables carrying HH may contrast with similar syllables carrying HL so these sequences must be regarded as phonemically distinct and, further, not simply as two variants of H linked to the occurrence of long vowels. Where it is necessary to mark tones on words the three sequences can be indicated as follows: HH as /"/, HL as /ˆ/ and LL as /"/. Tone will not be marked on the examples in the sections dealing with the morphology.

Syllables acquire length and sequences of tones in the following contexts:-

i) When a nominal (or noun) stem beginning with a vowel occurs with a prefix consisting of a consonant (C) or a consonant-cluster of the Cw- or Cy- type, usually as an alternative to a possible CV- prefix, the initial vowel of the stem is lengthened and carries a sequence of tones. These may be either LL or HH, the sequence LH becoming HH,

e.g. *l-`iba*   (dove) (5)   cp.[1]   *mà-ìbà*   (doves)   (6)
      m-űtwà (thorn) (3)   cp.   *mì-útwà*   (thorns) (4)

ii) When forms with initial syllabic nasals are initially inflected by an

---
[1] i.e. compare

inflecting morpheme with a short vowel, the vowel of the latter is lengthened and assumes the tone of the syllabic nasal. The nasal which is otherwise syllabic, becomes part of the syllabic margin of the following syllable. Such forms may be either nominal or verbal.

    e.g.   *ní- + -ǹjà*   >   *nî-njà*   (with a dog)

           nì- + -ǹsà   >   *nì-nsà*   (I am taking out)

           kù- + -ńgà   >   *kǔ-ngà*   (to take)

iii) The same effect is brought about when such forms occur in the middle of a phrase, e.g. as an object complement in a verb phrase,

    e.g.   *ànìlàtí + ǹjà*   >   *ànìlàtî – njà*   (I don't want a dog)

iv) Syllabic nasals occurring in sequences of identical shape,

    e.g.   *m̀mè*   (mother)   (1a)

           ǹnà   (I)

disappear in these contexts but nevertheless pass their tone to the preceding syllable.

    e.g.   *kí + m̀mè*   >   *kî-mè*   (it is mother)

           nìlà + m̀mè   >   *nìlàtâ-mè*   (I love mother)

Long vowels result from contraction of vowels. This happens when vowels without consonantal margins follow one another in the inflection of verb phrases. Opportunities for contraction are numerous as several of the subject prefixes, object prefixes and tense signs are V in form and many of the verb radicals are vowel-commencing. Contracted, and therefore long, vowels with tone sequences usually have alternatives in uncontracted forms.[1]

    e.g.   *Njà ìnè íhùhúlà*   ~   *ìné'hùhúlà*   (the dog was barking).

[1.] This section on tone and length is a summary of the clear treatment of the phenomena of tone and length in SiLozi in Gowlett 1964, pp. 8-9; 1967, pp. 5-11, 88-98.

MORPHOLOGY

The grammatical constructions of siLozi are of three kinds, **substantival, verbal** and **ideophonic**. They are each based upon a specific type of base or nucleus. In the case of the substantival constructions this nucleus is the **substantival stem**,

e.g.   *-tu* in /*mu-tu*/   (person)   (1)

In the case of the verbal constructions the nucleus is the **verb radical**, (or verb root),

e.g.   *-lat-* in /*a-ni-lat-i*/   (I don't want)

In the case of the ideophonic constructions the nucleus is the ideophone itself,

e.g.   *cwaa*   (being sour, of liquids)

The substantive stems, the verb radicals and the ideophones between them account for most of the entries in the lexicon or dictionary. A good number of the remainder are class or affix morphemes, i.e. prefixes, suffixes or infixes, which are needed to form constructions with the stems and radicals,

e.g.   *mu-* in /*mu-tu*/   (person)   (1)

         a-, ni-, -i in /*a-ni-lat-i*/   (I don't want)

Chapter 1
SUBSTANTIVAL CONSTRUCTIONS

The main types of substantive are the nouns, the pronouns, the demonstratives, the enumeratives, the selectors and the relatives. In this study the morphology of siLozi is presented as three hierarchies of constructions based, as already stated, on each of the three types of root morpheme, substantival, verbal and ideophonic. For example the description of the substantival hierarchy commences with the simplest constructions formed by combining affix morphemes with substantival stems as constituents. These constructions, namely the substantives, represent the **first level of substantival constructions.**

e.g.   *mu-tu*   (person)   (1)

The noun prefix of class 1 is one constituent and the noun stem /-*tu*/ is another.

Compare the following, all from Class I. Each exemplifies a different type of substantive, but all share a similar constructional pattern, namely affix + stem as two constituents.

e.g. (1)   *mu-tu*   (person)   (1)   noun
     (2)   *ye-na*   (he)   (1)   pronoun
     (3)   *y-ale*   (that yonder)   (1)   demonstrative
     (4)   *mu-ŋwí*   (one)   (1)   enumerative
     (5)   *u-fi?*   (which?)   (1)   selector
     (6.1) *yo-mu-hulu*   (big, grown up)   (1)   adjective
     (6.2) *yaa-butali*   (clever)   (1)   relative

The constructions at the first and simplest level are also constituents in more complex constructions at the **second level.** For example single substantives combine to form **substantive phrases** in which they are constrained to agree by means of affixes of the same class.

e.g.   *mutu yomuhulu*   (an adult person)   (1)

The noun headword, and the adjective agreeing with it in class, are the constituents of this construction. Other examples are:-

yona ifi?	(which one?)	(9)	pronoun + selector
musali yomuhulu	(an adult woman)	(1)	noun + adjective
mutu yo	(this person)	(1)	noun + demonstrative
yomuhulu ufi?	(which adult?)	(1)	adjective + selector
yaabutali yo	(this clever one)	(1)	relative +demonstrative

Constructions at the second level of complexity act as constituents at a **third level of construction**, namely that of the **inflected substantive phrase.** Here the constituents are the inflection on the one hand and the substantive phrase on the other. Inflections are of very different kinds, but they agree in the type of construction they form. They comprise the copulative inflection, which forms predicates; the possessive inflection which forms qualifying phrases; the adverbial inflection which forms adverbial complements in verb phrases; and subjectival inflections which also form predicates.

e.g.	*ki-mutu yomuhulu*	(it is an adult person)	cop. inflection
	ni-mutu yomuhulu	(with an adult person)	adv. inflection
	wa-mutu yomuhulu	(of an adult person)	poss. inflection
	ka-mulilo wo	(by means of this fire)	adv. inflection
	ki-mutu yo	(it is this person)	cop. inflection
	(mwana) wa-mutu yo	((the child) of this person) (1)	poss. inflection
	ni-mutu yomuhulu	(I am an adult person)	subj. inflection

A subsection of this level consists of subjectivally inflected relative stems,

e.g.	***u**-butali*	(he is clever)
	***ba**-teŋi*	(they are there)

One of these inflected substantival constructions, namely that with the copulative or predicative inflection /**ki-**/, acts as constituent at a **fourth level of**

construction, namely as the predicate in the **substantival clause.** The other constituent of the clause is the subject. Other inflected substantive phrases, e.g. those inflected by /**ni-**/, or by the possessive inflection, e.g. /**wa-**/, are constituents in other types of construction.

e.g.   *Mubanga kimutu yomuhulu*   (Mubanga is an adult person)
'*Mubanga*' is the subject and '*kimutu yomuhulu*' is the predicate of this substantival clause.

Mutu yo umusa   This person is kind

'*Muto yo*' is the subject and '*umusa*' is the predicate of this substantival clause.

A fifth level of substantival constructions is that of the sentence. In such a construction there is a principal clause which is substantival. It is accompanied by one or more clauses, either principal or subordinate.

This system of analysing constructions in terms of their constituents, constructions which become in turn constituents in more complex constructions at higher and higher levels, is applied to the verbal constructions based on verb radicals and, to a lesser extent, to those based on ideophones. Such a description affords an insight into the way in which siLozi speakers form their clauses and sentences which are the important units of communication.

LEVEL I : THE SUBSTANTIVE

THE NOUN

(a) Typically nouns are constructed according to the following pattern:
    class prefix + noun stem

(b) There are 17 class prefixes in siLozi which combine with noun stems to form nouns. These class prefixes are given below. They are numbered according to the system used in the comparative study of Bantu languages which shows the extent to which siLozi fits in with the general Bantu pattern and what is its own individual character.

Singular		**No Number**		**Plural**	
1.	mu-			2.	ba-
1a.	Ø- (zero prefix)			2a.	bo-
3.	mu-			4.	mi-
5.	li-			6.	ma-
7.	si-			8.	bi-
9.	N-			10.9	liN-
				10.	li-
11.	lu-				
12.	ka-			13.	tu-
		14.	bu-		
		15.	ku-		
		16.	(fa-)		
		17.	ku-		
		18.	(mu-)		

(c) Nouns with the same class prefix in common form a noun class. Thus, for example,

e.g.   *mu-tú*   (person); and
       mu-sáli   (woman)

are both nouns of class 1, having the prefix /mu-/ of class 1 in common.

(d) The prefix of class 1a is /Ø-/ or zero. Nouns in this class share in common the feature of having no prefix. In a system where the nouns of all other classes do have overt class prefixes, this absence is significant and serves as a class mark.

e.g.   *ndate*   (father)   (1a)

        mma   (mother)   (1a)

(e) Most prefixes convey either singular number or plural. As listed they are paired, unevenly numbered prefixes up to 11 being singular and the corresponding evenly numbered prefixes being plural,

e.g.   *mu-tu*   (person)   (1)

        ba-tu   (persons, people)   (2)

However, the plural prefix corresponding to that of class 11 is /*ma-*/ (6) and class 12 prefix /*ka-*/ and class 13 prefix /*lu-*/ are singular and plural respectively. The plural of class 9 nouns is formed by adding class 10 prefix to that of class 9, not substituting it as is the general rule. Class 10 prefix is usually substituted for that of class 7 to form its plurals. The class prefixes of classes 16 and 18 are not constituents of nouns but of other substantival constructions.

The Noun Classes

Class prefix 1 is /*mu-*/ before consonant commencing stems.

e.g.   *mu-sali*   (woman)   (1)

The prefix is /*mw-*/ before some stems commencing with vowels.

e.g.   *mw-ana*   (child)   (1)

        mw-enyi   (visitor)   (1)

It is singular in number. Its regular correlative plural is class prefix 2, /*ba-*/. In some cases class 1 nouns form plurals with class prefix 6.

e.g.   ma-Lozi   (the Lozi people) (6)   cp.   mu-Lozi   (a Lozi person) (1)

Nouns in class 1 all indicate singular human beings of various kinds, tribes and conditions.

Class Prefix 2 is /*ba-*/. It is /*b-*/ before some stems commencing in /*a*/.

e.g.   ba-sali   (women)   (2)
       b-ana   (children)   (2)

Class 2 nouns indicate the plural of the correlative class 1 forms.

Class prefix 1a is /*Ø-*/. Overtly, nouns of class 1a consist only of a stem.

e.g.   ndate   (father)   (1a)
       mme   (mother)   (1a)

Nouns with class 1a prefix indicate kinship terms, personal names, some names of animals and personifications.

Class prefix 2a is /*bo-*/. Substituted for class 1a prefix it forms plurals of number.

e.g.   bo-ndate   (fathers)   (2a)
       bo-mme   (mothers)   (2a)   cp.   bo-mma   (my mother) (2a)

When prefixed to some class 1 nouns, honorific plurals are formed.

e.g.   Bo-Mukwae   (Honourable Princess) (2a)

When prefixed to personal names, the plural meaning may be either honorific or numerical.

e.g.   bo-Sitali   (the Sitalis, or Mr. Sitali)

Class prefix 3 is /*mu-*/ before consonant-commencing stems.

e.g.   *mu-nwana*   (finger)   (3)

It is /*mw-*/ or /*m-*/ before certain stems commencing with vowels.

e.g.   *mw-aha*   (year)   (3)
       mw-endano   (race)   (3)
       mw-ila   (taboo)   (3)
       m-oyo   (heart)   (3)
       m-utwa   (thorn)   (3)

Nouns with class prefix 3 are singular and form plurals with class prefix 4, /*mi-*/.

Class 3 nouns with primary prefix /*mu-*/ indicate the names of many trees and plants, some animals, parts of the body and miscellanea. When used as a secondary prefix, viz. when substituted for prefixes other than their correlative plurals, it is augmentative and pejorative.

e.g.   *mu-lundu*   (steep, difficult hill) (3)   cp.   *li-lundu*   (hill) (5)

The primary prefixes of a noun stem are those with which it is used to indicate items as normal specimens of their kind. Prefixes become secondary when they are substituted for primary prefixes in order to convey implications which portray items as abnormal or out of the ordinary in some specific way, for example as large, small, awkward, unpleasant and so on.

Class prefix 4 is /*mi-*/.

e.g.   *mi-nwana*   (fingers)   (4)

It is /*my-*/ before some stems commencing in vowels

e.g. *my-aha*   ~   *mi-aha*   (years)   (4)
      my-oyo   ~   *mi-oyo*   (hearts) (4)
      mi-utwa   (thorns) (4)

Class 4 nouns indicate the plural of the correlative class 3 forms.

Class prefix 5 is /li-/.

e.g.   *li-cwe*   (stone)

It is /l-/ before some stems commencing with /i/, and /ly-/ before some stems commencing with /o, u/.

e.g. *l-ino*   ~   *li-ino*   (tooth)   (5)
      l-ito   ~   *li-ito*   (eye)   (5)
      ly-omba ~   *li-omba* (kind of fishing net) (5)

Class 5 contains the names of many things found in pairs, e.g. parts of the body, or in plenty, e.g. the animals that go in herds, fruit found in abundance. As a secondary prefix it is augmentative.

e.g.   *li-sali*   (big woman)

Class prefix 6 is /ma-/

e.g.   *ma-cwe*   (stones)

The vowel of the prefix coalesces with the initial vowel of stems commencing in /a/ and the stems /-*ino*/ (tooth), /-*ito*/ (eye)

e.g.   *meno*   (teeth)   (6)
       meto   (eyes)   (6)
       m-anda   (bundles) (6)

Nouns of class 5 and 11 have correlative plurals in class 6.

e.g. *ma-naka* (horns) (6) cp. *lu-naka* (horn) (11)

In addition to containing plural nouns with the general meanings of classes 5 and 11, class 6 contains a number of nouns of no number indicating the names of liquids. A number of class 1 nouns indicating tribal, national or racial affiliation form plurals of class 6.

e.g. *ma-Lozi* (the Lozi people) (6)
cp. *mu-Lozi* (a member of the Lozi people) (1)

A number of class 9 nouns form plurals in class 6.

e.g. *ma-simu* (fields) (6)
cp. *simu* (field) (9)

Class prefix 7 is /si-/

e.g. *si-fuba* (chest)
si-oli (island)
si-ulwi (red ant)

It is /s-/ with certain vowel-commencing stems.

e.g. *s-ongo* (piece of iron) (7)

Class 7 contains the names of many material objects, sicknesses, things or persons that are imperfect and fall short, styles of acting and speaking. As a secondary prefix[1] it is pejorative and often augmentative.

e.g. *si-saka* (rough old sack) (7) cp. *saka* (sack) (9)
si-ongolo (big insect)

As a rule primary class 7 nouns form correlative plurals in class 10. Secondary

---

[1] Secondary prefixes are those which are substituted for primary prefixes when it is designed to convey implications that indicate items as abnormal or out of the ordinary.

class 7 nouns form plurals in class 8.

	e.g.	si-hwana	(calabash)	(7)
		li-hwana	(calabashes)	(10)
but		si-zeve	(big ear)	(7)
		bi-zeve	(big ears)	(8)

Class prefix 8 is /bi-/

e.g.	bi-ongolo	(big insects)
	bi-utu	(big clumsy feet)

It is /by-/ with certain vowel-commencing stems.

e.g.	by-ongo	(pieces of iron)

This class provides correlative plurals for secondary nouns of classes 7 and 11.

Class prefix 9 is /N-/, a homorganic nasal.

e.g.   n-ja

The prefix /n/ is only found overtly with monosyllabic stems. In all other cases its presence is hidden, but its influence is shown by the sound changes it causes when prefixed to certain consonant-commencing stems.

e.g.	pina	(song)	(9)	cp.	-bin-	(sing)
	tau	(lion)	(9)			
	namani	(calf)	(9)			

Class 9 contains many names of animals and of many objects of everyday life. The plurals of class 9 nouns are usually in class 10.9 though some form their plurals in class 6.

e.g.	li-n-ja	(dogs)	(10.9)

ma-namani (calves) (6.9)

With monosyllabic stems /N-/ is homorganic being /m, n, ny and ŋ/ before labial, alveolar, palatal and velar commencing stems respectively.

e.g. m-pye (ostrich) (9)
 n-du (house) (9)
 n-ja (dog) (9)
 n-gu [ŋ-gu] (sheep) (9)

In the case of certain consonants at the beginning of stems, the prefixing of /N-/ causes a morphophonemic change, that is a change in the phonemic shape of the morpheme. When the stem is monosyllabic /N-/ also appears as a syllabic nasal. In the case of longer stems /N-/ consists of the sound change. These changes, which seem confined to nominal constructions based on verb radicals, may be summarised as follows:

Stem commencing consonants /b-/, /f-/, /l-/, /h-/ and /V-[1]/ become /p-/, /p-/, /t-/, /k-/ and /kV-/ respectively.

e.g. N + -buz- (ask) + -o become puzo (question)
 N + -f- (give) + -o " mpo (gift)
 N + -lut- (teach) + -o " tuto (lesson)
 N + -han- (deny) + -o " kano (denial)
 N + -alab- (answer) + -o " kalabo (answer)

Class prefix 10 is /li-/:

Class 10 prefix /li-/ is substituted for the class 7 prefix /si-/ when the latter is a primary prefix in order to form correlative plurals.

e.g. li-fuba (chests) (10)

---
[1] i.e. a vowel

    li-oli   (islands)   (10)

Together with class prefix 9 /*N-*/, it forms correlative plurals of class 9 nouns.

e.g.   *li-n-ga*   (dogs)   (10.9)
      li-tau   (lions)   (10.9)
      li-m-pye   (ostriches)   (10.9)
      li-n-gu   (sheep)   (10.9)
      li-puzo   (questions)   (10.9)
      li-m-po   (gifts)   (10.9)
      li-tuto   (lessons)   (10.9)
      li-kano   (denials)   (10.9)
      li-kalabo   (answers)   (10.9)

Class prefix 11 is /*lu-*/.

e.g.   *lu-naka*   (horn)

It occurs as /*lw-*/ before certain stems commencing in /*a, e, i*/

e.g.   *lw-aa*   (reed mat for bottom of canoe) (11)
      lw-enge   (white of egg)   (11)

and as /*l-*/ before certain stems commencing in /*o, u*/.

e.g.   *l-oya*   (single soft hair)   (11)

Class 11 is singular and contains the names of things characterised by length as well as many miscellanea. Secondary nouns are characterised by implications of length or thinness. Plurals of secondary class 11 nouns are in class 8.

e.g.   *lu-ngo*   (sharp, pointed nose)   (11)   cp. *bi-ngo*   (sharp noses) (8)
      lu-zebe   (long ear)   (11)   cp. *bi-zebe*   (long ears)   (8)

Prefix 11 with stems indicating grains, plants and crops indicates one single stem or specimen.

e.g. *lu-cwaɲi* (one blade of grass) (11)

Class prefix 12 is /*ka-*/,

e.g. *ka-banze* (scorpion) (12)

It is /*k-*/ before stems commencing with /a/.

e.g. *k-ana* (small child) (12)

Nouns in class 12 are singular and include a number of miscellaneous things, sometimes with unpleasant connotations. Secondary nouns in class 12 indicate diminutives and things which are unpleasant or a nuisance.

e.g. *ka-mbuki* (young, feeble diviner) (12)
      ka-loyawe (old garden cursed long ago and which people will not cultivate)

Class prefix 13 is /*tu-*/

e.g. *tu-banze* (scorpions) (13)
      tu-ungu (undersized pumpkins) (13) cp. *kaungu* (undersized pumpkin) (12)

It is /*tw-*/ before stems commencing in /a/

e.g. *tw-ana* (small children)

Nouns in class 13 are plural and convey the meanings of their correlative singular.

Class prefix 14 is /*bu-*/

e.g. *bu-sihu* (night)

   bu-cwaŋi (grass)

It is /*bw*/ before stems commencing in /*a, e, i*/

e.g. *bwanyu* (good luck, e.g. in spearing of fish) (14)

and /*b*/ before /*o, u*/

e.g. *boya* (hair, wool, down)

Class 14 contains the names of substances or things found in mass. Secondary nouns of class 14 indicate names of countries or abstract qualities,

e.g. *bu-nunu* (many fleas)
   bu-Lozi (Lozi-land)
   bu-tu   (humanity)

Class 15 prefix is /*ku-*/

This prefix is used along with terminal vowel /*a-*/ in the infinitive inflection of verb phrases,

e.g. *ku-bon-a batu* (to see people)
   ku-f-a mpo (to give a gift)

Class 17 prefix is /*ku-*/

This prefix is used with nouns and pronouns to form locative nouns or nominal constructions in which a place is designated with general reference to the person or object to which /*ku-*/ is prefixed.

e.g. *ku-mulena* (where the chief is)
   ku-bona (where they are)

The class prefixes of class 16 and class 18, /*fa-*/ and /*mu-*/, occur in substantival constructions other than nouns and nominal constructions.

NOMINAL CONSTRUCTIONS

The noun class prefixes combine with stems other than simple noun stems consisting of one morpheme. Such stems may be complex and made up of combinations of substantival, verbal or ideophonic morphemes. They may also be simplex (i.e. without affixes) yet taken from a class other than that of the noun stems.

Complex Nominal Stems

(a) stems and diminutive suffixes /-*nyana*, -*ana*/

e.g.	*tau-nyana*	(little lion)	(9)	cp.	*tau*	(lion)	(9)
	silepe-nyana	(little axe)	(7)	cp.	*silepe*	(axe)	(7)
	musali-nyana	(little woman)	(1)	cp.	*musali*	(woman)	(1)

(b) stems and augmentative suffix /-*tota*/

e.g. *munna-tota* (a real man)
      tau-tota   (a huge lion)

(c) reduplicated stems

e.g.	*mufili-fili*	(trouble)	(3)
	kacima-cima	(irritableness)	(12)
	sico seo simunati-nati	(that food is very pleasant)	(3)

Nominal Constructions based on Verb Radicals

In these constructions the prefix appears to combine with terminal vowels to form one constituent, the verb radicals being the other.

| e.g. | *mu-lim-i* | (farmer) | (1) | cp. | *-lim-* | (cultivate) |
| | *bu-pil-o* | (health) | (14) | cp. | *-pil-* | (live) |

si-tahw-a   (drunkard)   (7)   cp.   *-tahw-*   (become drunk)

Nominal Constructions based on Ideophones
e.g. *ngele-ngele*   (hand bell)   cp.   *ngele*   (ringing)
   sikwakwakwa   (machine gun)   cp.   *kwa*   (report of gun)

Nominal Constructions of Class 1a with prefixal formatives /*i-*/ (often masculine) and /*na-*/ (often feminine) are common in the dictionary.

e.g. *imatala*   (someone who never has enough food)   (1a)
   imukuka   (one who does not take care of his belongings)   (1a)
   namukuka   (untidy woman)   (1a)
   namulomo   (talkative woman)   (1a)

Nominal Constructions of Class 2a occur when the prefix /*bo-*/ is used as constituent with a phrase.

e.g. *bo-ndat' amina*   (your fathers)
   bo-ndat' aluna   (our fathers)
   bo-ndat' abona   (their fathers)

Nominal constructions are formed by the use of secondary prefixes with complex stems made up of the morpheme /*nga*/ and nouns of class 1a or 2a.

e.g. *ka-nga-Sitali*   (the little Sitali)
   tu-nga-boSitali   (the little Sitalis)

THE PRONOUN

Constructional pattern:

Person or class affix (+ -o-, classes 2 to 18 only) + stabiliser /**na-**/. The stabiliser /-**na**/ fulfils a mainly phonological role in enabling the pronoun to function as a phonological word of two syllables with the accent on penultimate length.

The forms of the person and class affixes in pronouns with incidence of /-o-/ and the stabiliser are shown in the following table.

			Singular		**No number**		**Plural**
I			*n-na*				*lu-na*
II			*we-na*				*mi-na*
III¹	class	1.	*ye-na*			2.	*b-o-na*
		3.	*w-o-na*			4.	*y-o-na*
		5.	*l-o-na*			6.	*ø-o-na*
		7.	*s-o-na*			8.	*by-o-na*
		9.	*y-o-na*			10.	*z-o-na*
		11.	*l-o-na*				
		12.	*k-o-na*			13.	*t-o-na*
				14.	*b-o-na*		
				15.	*k-o-na*		
				16.	*f-o-na*		
				17.	*k-o-na*		
				18.	*m-o-na*		

The pronoun contributes emphasis or prominence especially when it is used in appositional phrases or in contrast. When inflected, pronouns lose their emphatic references.

e.g.   *Luna lufitile kanako, bona*   (**We** arrived in time, **they** were late)
        nebaliehile

---
[1] i.e. First, second and third person

but	*lico za-luna*	(our food,)	
	Mulena yena wabulela	(**The chief** is talking; it is the chief who is talking)	
but	*Nenisabuleli niyena*	(I was not speaking with him)	
	mina maLozi	(you Lozi)	(II, 6)
	yena ndate	(my father himself)	(1)
	wona munzi	(the village itself)	(3)
	bona bucwaŋi	(the grass itself)	(14)
	fona foo	(that very place)	(16)

THE DEMONSTRATIVES

There are four series of demonstratives with the following constructional patterns:

Series 1 : Demonstrative class affix + a secondary vowel /**-o**/, /**-e**/ or /**-a**/, depending on whether the class has vowel /**-u**/, /**-i**/ or /**-a**/ in its noun prefix   (here)

Series 2 : Demonstrative class affix + secondary vowel + /**-o**/   (there)

Series 3 :
Series 4 :   Demonstrative class affix + stems /**-ale**/ or /**-ani**/   (yonder).

		1	2	3	4
Class	1	*y-o*	*y-o-o*	*y-ale*	*y-ani*
	2	*b-a*	*b-a-o*	*b-ale*	*b-ani*
	3	*w-o*	*w-o-o*	*w-ale*	*w-ani*
	4	*y-e*	*y-e-o*	*y-ale*	*y-ani*

	1	2	3	4
5	l-e	l-e-o	l-ale	l-ani
6	ø-a	ø-a-o	ø-ale	ø-ani
7	s-e	s-e-o	s-ale	s-ani
8	by-e	by-e-o	by-ale	by-ani
9	y-e	y-e-o	y-ale	y-ani
10	z-e	z-e-o	z-ale	z-ani
11	l-o	l-o-o	lw-ale	lw-ani
12	k-a	k-a-o	k-ale	k-ani
13	t-o	t-o-o	tw-ale	tw-ani
14	b-o	b-o-o	bw-ale	bw-ani
15	k-o	k-o-o	kw-ale	kw-ani
16	f-a	f-o-o	f-ale	f-ani
17	kw-ana	k-o-o	kw-ale	kw-ani
18	m-o	m-o-o	mw-ale	mw-ani

Note that the first position demonstrative of class 17 is irregular and that in the 3rd and 4th position, alternative forms of the class affix of classes 11, 13, 14, 15, 17 and 18 occur of Cw[1] shape, this being required as a margin to the stems which commence in /a/.

The demonstrative of first position indicates objects near to the speaker, those of second position objects near the hearer, and those of the third and fourth positions, which have no difference in meaning, objects at a distance from both speaker and hearer.

e.g. *yo*   (this one)   (1)   e.g. *mutu*   (person)   (1)
     ze   (these ones) (10)   *linja* (dogs)   (10)

---
[1] i.e. Consonant followed by w

yeo	(that one)	(9)		buka	(book)	(9)
yani	(that one yonder)	(9)		kota	(tree)	(9)
wale	(that one yonder)	(3)		munzi	(village)	(3)

THE ENUMERATIVE

The constructional pattern:

    enumerative prefix + enumerative stem

The forms of the class affixes as enumerative prefixes are as follows:

1.	mu-		2.	ba-
3.	mu-		4.	mi-
5.	li-		6.	ma-
7.	si-		8.	bi-
9.	ŋ-		10.	li-
11.	lu-			
12.	ka-		13.	tu-
		14.	bu-	
		15.	ku-	
		17.	ku-	

The enumerative stems are:

    -ŋwi   (one)

    -ɲi?   (of what kind?)   (classes 1 and 6 only)

Stem /-ŋwi/ does not occur with the class affixes of plural classes, save with that of class 2 with honorific meaning.

e.g.   bondate bali baŋwi   (father on his own)

Enumeratives with stem /-ŋwi/ (one) are always used as complements of the verb /-li/ (be) in participial[1] phrases.

---

[1] i.e. phrases involving a participle

e.g. *busihu buli buŋwi*   (only one night)
     mutu ali muŋwi   (only one person)
     komu ili ŋŋwi   (only one ox)

The enumerative stem /-ŋi?/ is commonly only used in classes 1 and 6 and, as selector stem, in class 9.

THE SELECTOR

Constructional pattern:
    selector prefix + selector stem

The forms of the class affixes as selector prefixes are as follows:

1.	u-	2.	ba-
3.	u-	4.	i-
5.	li-	6.	a-
7.	si-	8.	bi-
9.	i-	10.	li-
11.	lu-		
12.	ka-	13.	tu-
14.	bu-		
15.	ku-		
17.	ku-		

The selector stems are:
    -fi?   (which one?)
    -ŋi?   (of what kind?)   (class 9 only)
    -sili   (different)
e.g. *mutu ufi?*   (which person?)   (1)

munzi usili   (a different village)   (3)

ŋja iŋi?   (a dog of what sex?)   (9)

THE RELATIVES

SiLozi, like other Sotho languages, has a number of relatively inflected constructions which occur in substantive phrases either as headwords or qualifiers. As constructions the relatives belong to the analytical level of the inflected substantives or substantive phrases. Since, however, these constructions are normally rankshifted as secondary members of the constituent class of substantive in substantive phrases, and since it is customary to treat relatives and adjectives among the substantives, their treatment is anticipated here to some extent.

There are three types of relative construction distinguished according to the set of relative inflecting morphemes which are used. These are:
(i) relative inflected adjectives
(ii) relative inflected stems and verb phrases
(iii) relative inflected verbal clauses.

RELATIVE INFLECTED ADJECTIVES

Constructional pattern:
    relative prefix (1) + adjective

The constructional pattern of the adjective is:
    adjectival prefix + adjectival stem.

The adjectival prefixes are the same in form as the noun prefixes save that class 10 prefix does not occur, that of class 9 being used for both class 9 and 10.

e.g. *tau ye-ŋŋwi* (another lion) (9) cp. *-ŋwi* (another)
    litau ze-peli (two lions) (10.9) cp. *-beli* (two)
    ndu ye-nde (a pleasant house) (9) cp. *-nde* (pleasant)
    lipalisa ze-nde (pleasant flowers) (10.9)

Further, the adjectival prefixes of classes 16 and 18 are not used, that of class 17 being used instead with the relative prefixes of classes 16 and 18.

e.g. *fo-ku-nde* (at a nice place)
    mo-ku-nde (in a nice place)
    fo-ku-nsu (at the black part)
    mo-ku-fubelu (in the red part)

Apart from their use in nominal constructions sometimes used as praise names,
e.g. *mali-mabi* (bad luck) cp. *mali amaswe* (bad blood)
adjectives are used only in an inflected form, the inflection being the **relative class affix**,
e.g. *yomunde* (one who is pleasant (a relative inflected adjective))

The relative class affixes which inflect adjectives are called series (1) and **they** are the same in form as the demonstratives 1st position save in the cases of classes 3, 16 and 17.

The following table of forms illustrates the forms of the relative class **affixes** and the adjectival prefixes as used with the adjective stem /**-nde**/ (nice, good).

	Singular		**No number**		**Plural**
1.	yo-mu-nde			2.	ba-ba-nde
3.	o-mu-nde			4.	ye-mi-nde
5.	le-li-nde			6.	a-ma-nde
7.	se-si-nde			8.	bye-bi-nde
9.	ye-ø-nde			10.	ze-ø-nde
11.	lo-lu-nde				
12.	ka-ka-nde			13.	to-tu-nde
		14.	bo-bu-nde		
		15.	ko-ku-nde		
		16.	fo-ku-nde		
		17.	ko-ku-nde		
		18.	mo-ku-nde		

The adjective stems in siLozi number some thirty of which over half refer to the colours and patterns on markings of cattle.

e.g.

-nca	(young, new)	*-hulu*	(adult, old)
-kuswani	(short)	*-telele*	(tall, long)
-sisani	(thin, slender, lean)	*-kima*	(stout, thick)
-nyinyani	(small, few)	*-ŋata*	(much, many)
-kana	(so many)	*-kai?*	(how many?, how much?)
-sihali	(female)	*-tuna*	(big, male)
-nde	(nice, good)	*-cupya*	(hornless)
		-supya	(hornless)
-beli	(two)	*-lalu*	(three)
-ne	(four)	*-ŋwi*	(another, others)

The adjective stems may be freely used with any of the class affixes.

Examples of relative inflected adjectives

yo-mu-nde	(a good one)	(1)	e.g.	*mutu*	(person)	(1)
ba-ba-nca	(young ones)	(2)	e.g.	*batu*	(people)	(2)
o-mu-telele	(a long one)	(3)	e.g.	*mukwakwa*	(road)	(3)
ye-mi-nyinyani	(small ones)	(4)	e.g.	*minzi*	(villages)	(4)
ye-mi-ŋwi	(others)	(4)	e.g.	*minzi*	(villages)	(4)
le-li-sisani	(a thin one)	(5)	e.g.	*lizoho*	(arm)	(5)
a-ma-kai?	(how many?)	(6)	e.g.	*mazazi*	(days)	(6)
se-si-nde	(a nice one)	(7)	e.g.	*sikolo*	(school)	(7)
bye-bi-beli	(two)	(8)	e.g.	*biemba*	(fragments)	(8)
ye-tuna	(an old one)	(9)	e.g.	*kwena*	(crocodile)	(9)
ze-talu	(three)	(10.9)	e.g.	*litapi*	(fish)	(10)

The adjectives indicating colour have complex forms with suffix /-*ana*/ when applied to female animals.

e.g.	*ye-swana*	(a black female one)	(9)	viz.	*komu*	(cow) (9)
cp.	*ye-nsu*	(a black male one)	(9)	viz.	*komu*	(cow) (9)

The construction adjective stem + /-*ana*/ is accompanied by a number of morphophonemic changes (cp. Jalla, 1937, p. 21).

RELATIVE INFLECTED STEMS

Constructional pattern:
    relative prefix (2) + relative stem

The relative stems in question here may be inflected, principally or relatively by the addition of the correct inflecting person or class affix.

e.g. *ba-buzwa* (they are lazy, e.g. batho (people)) (2) (principally)
baba-buzwa (they who are lazy) (2) (relatively)
li-boi (they are cowardly, e.g. *linja* (dogs)) (10) (principally)
zee-boi (they who are cowardly) (10) (relatively)

Many of the stems which are inflected in this way are nouns,

e.g. *buzwa* (laziness) (14)

The following table shows the relative prefixes which are used with relative stems. They constitute series (2) of the relative class affixes.

	Singular		**No number**		**Plural**
1.	*yaa-*			2.	*baba-*
3.	*woo-*			4.	*yee-*
5.	*leli-*			6.	*aa-*
7.	*sesi-*			8.	*byebi-*
9.	*yee-*			10.	*zee-*
11.	*lolu*				
12.	*kaka-*			13.	*totu-*
		14.	*bobu-*		
		15.	*koku-*		
		17.	*koku-*		

These prefixes are also used to inflect verb phrases.

e.g.	*linja zee-zuma hande*	(dogs which hunt well)
cp.	*linja zi-zuma hande*	(dogs hunt well)
e.g.	*batho baba-bona hande*	(people who see well)
cp.	*batho ba-bona hande*	(people see well)
e.g.	*mucaha yaa-seha hahulu*	(a young man who laughs loudly)
cp.	*mucaha useha hahulu*	(the young man is laughing loudly)

The following is a list of relative stems in common use:

-boi	(cowardly)	cp.	*boi*	(cowardice)	(14)
-bukiti	(heavy)		*bukiti*	(weight)	(14)
-bunolo	(soft, easy)		*bunolo*	(softness)	(14)
-buhali	(angry)		*buhali*	(anger)	(14)
-buŋala	(stubborn)		*buŋala*	(stubbornness)	(14)
-cwalo	(like that)		*cwalo*	(in that way)	(adv.)
-cwana	(like this)		*cwana*	(thus)	(adv.)
-liti	(blunt)				
-fufu	(warm)				
-koopo	(crooked, dishonest)				
-lubilo	(fast)		*lubilo*	(speed)	(11)
-mapuna	(naked)		*mapunu*	(nakedness)	(6)
-maswe	(bad)		*maswe*	(evil)	(6)
-mata	(strong)		*mata*	(strength)	(6)
-mezi	(wet)		*mezi*	(water)	(6)
-munati	(delicious)		*munati*	(good taste)	(3)
-musa	(kind, good)		*musa*	(mercy)	(3)
-sipala	(broad)				
-taba	(wild)				
-tata	(hard, difficult)		*tata*	(difficulty)	(9)

e.g. *linja zee-buhali* (savage dogs) (10)
      mucaha yaa-mata (a strong young man) (1)
      pizi yee-lubilo (a swift horse) (9)
      kokumezi (at a wet place) (17)

Negative forms of the relative inflected stems are formed by prefixing the negative sign /-*si*-/ to the relative stem.

e.g. *mucaha yaa-si-cwalo*   (a young man who is not like that)

Where, however, the relative stems are nouns they become complements of a verb phrase with radical /-*na*/ (be with) which is negatively inflected.

e.g. *linja zee-si-na buhali*   (dogs which are not fierce; lit. which do not have fierceness).

pizi yee-si-na lubilo   (a horse which does not have swiftness).

Negative relative forms of all substantives are formed by prefixing this negative relative inflection, viz. relative prefix (2) + /-*si*-/.

e.g. *mwana yaa-si-yomunde*   (a child who is not good)
batu baba-si-bao   (people who are not those ones)
nama yee-si-yahau   (meat which is not yours)

RELATIVE INFLECTED CLAUSES

Participial verbal clauses are inflected to enable them to refer to substantives.

e.g. *mutu yenenibona*   (the person whom I was seeing)
cp. *nenibona mutu*   (I was seeing the person)
e.g. *linja ze-muboni*   (the dogs you saw)
cp. *muboni linja*   (you saw the dogs)

The constructional pattern of these constructions is as follows:
  Relative affix (3) + clause

The following table shows the relative affixes which are used to inflect verbal clauses. They constitute series (3) of the relative class affixes.

	Singular		No number		Plural
1.	ye-			2.	be-
3.	o-			4.	ye-
5.	le-			6.	a-
7.	se-			8.	bye-
9.	ye-			10.	ze-
11.	lo-				
12.	ke-			13.	to-
		14.	bo-		
		15.	ko-		
		16.	fo-		
		17.	ko-		
		18.	mo-		

The vowels of these affixes are elided before the subject prefixes of class 1 or class 6, /*a-*/.

e.g. *b-abona* (those whom he sees) (2) e.g. *batu* (people) (2)
    ye-mubona (the one you see) (1) e.g. *mutu* (person) (1)
    ye-neniŋola (the one I was writing) (9) e.g. *buka* (book) (9)
    fo-niyahile (where I dwell) (16) e.g. *fasibaka* (at the place) (16)

    kinna ye-uziba (It is I whom you know) (1)
    Kiluna bao be-muziba (We are those whom you know) (2)

LEVEL II : THE SUBSTANTIVE PHRASES

Substantives of all kinds combine to form constructions at the next level of complexity, viz. substantive phrases. Constructional pattern:

nuclear substantive + substantive(s) in agreement

The two aspects mentioned in the constructional pattern are of importance. A phrase must consist of at least two substantives and these must be in agreement. The term substantive is the name of a constituent class whose primary members are the various types of substantive, i.e. nouns, pronouns, demonstratives, enumeratives and selectors and which has secondary members as well e.g. the relative constructions. Secondary members are those constructions which belong as constructions to levels other than that of the substantive, but which function as substantives by rank-shifting.

Examples of substantive phrases

sona sibatana seo	(that same animal) (7) (pronoun, noun, demonstrative (2))
nja yona yeo	(that very dog) (9) (noun, pronoun, demonstrative (2))
litaba zeo	(those matters) (10) (noun, demonstrative (2))
nja iŋi?	(a dog of what sex?) (9) (noun, selector)
nja ifi?	(which dog?) (9) (noun, selector)
bao basili	(those different ones) (2) (demonstrative (2), selector)
bana babanca	(young children) (2) (noun, relative adjective)
myaha yemiŋata	(many years) (4) (noun, relative adjective)

sipulumuki sesifubelu	(a red butterfly) (7) (noun, relative adjective)
tipa yeebuliti	(a blunt knife) (9) (noun, relative inflected stem)
munna yaamata	(a strong man) (1) (noun, relative inflected stem)
hona mo	(in there) (17, 18) (pronoun, demonstrative (1))

While it is necessary to define a substantive phrase (SP) as substantive + substantive in agreement at the level of the SP, it is useful for reasons of economy in description to define it a little more widely when it occurs as a constituent in larger constructions, viz. as substantive +/- substantive in agreement. This means that the term SP as a constituent includes both substantives and substantive phrases. For example in the construction "inflected SP", whose constructional pattern is:

inflection + SP

the term SP may include both phrases and individual substantives as members of the constituent class of SP.

e.g. *nimutu yomuhulu* (with a senior person)
     nimutu (with a person)

Both these constructions are inflected SPs. In the first example the SP is a phrase consisting of two substantival constructions in agreement. In the second the SP is a single substantive without accompanying substantives in agreement.

COMPOUND PHRASES

Phrases may be combined either (i) in apposition or (ii) as formed by conjunctives.

e.g. (i) *basali kaufela* (all the women)
        likomu kaufela (all the oxen)

	musizana ndiala	(a girl orphan)
(ii)	*bomme ni-bondate*	(mother and father)
	bomme kapa bondate	(mother or father)

LEVEL III : THE INFLECTED SUBSTANTIVE PHRASES

Substantive phrases are inflected as such by prefixing the following inflecting morphemes.

(1) copulative /*ki-*/ (it is), *hasi* (it is not)

(2) subjective, e.g. /*ki-*/ (I)

(3) adverbial, e.g. /*ka-*/ (by means of);
/*ni-*/ (with)

(4) possessive class affix + /*-a-*/ (of)

The result is a substantival construction of level III with constructional pattern:
inflecting morpheme + SP

COPULATIVE PHRASES

Copulative phrases inflected by /*ki-*/ (it is)

(a) Affirmative copulative phrases are formed by prefixing the inflecting morpheme /*ki-*/ to substantive phrases, e.g.

ki-mutu yomuhulu	(it is a senior person)	cp. *mutu yomuhulu* (1)
ki-yena yo	(it is this one himself)	cp. *yena yo* (1)
ki-bao babansu	(it is those black ones)	cp. *bao babansu* (2)
ki-ali muŋwi fela	(it is the only one)	cp. *ali muŋwi fela* (1)

ki-ufi?	(it is which one?)	cp. *ufi?*	(1)
ki-yomunde yoo	(it is that pleasant one)	cp. *yomunde yoo*	(1)
ki-zetuna zensu	(it is the big black ones)	cp. *zetuna zensu*	(10)
ki-yaamusa	(it is the kind one)	cp. *yaamusa*	(1)
ki-zeebuhali zenyinyani	(it is the small angry ones)	cp. *zeebuhali zenyinyani*	(10)

(b) Copulative phrases belong to the constituent class of adjuncts in verb phrases. In passive extended verb phrases they indicate the agents by which the action was done. See p. 62 for a description of adjuncts as constituents in verb phrases.

e.g. *Nenishwezi **ki-kaizeli yaka***   (I was bereaved of my sister)
      *Nenitabilwe **ki-komu yetuna***   (I was gored by a big ox)
      *Nenilatehezi **ki-mali yenata***   (I suffered the loss of a large sum of money)
      *Neninatilwe **ki-ndate yomuhulu***   (I was beaten by my father's elder brother)

(c) The negative inflection of SPs is /**hasi**/.

e.g. *hasi mutu yomuhulu*   (it is not a senior person)

(d) SPs consisting of an infinitive inflected verb phrase are among those copulatively inflected, by /**ki-**/.

e.g. *Hasi kuhalifa. Ki-kubapala fela*   (It is not anger. It is only play)
      Ki-kuli akaipulukela lico zahae anosi?   (Is it that he can keep all his food to himself?)

Copulative Phrases Inflected by Subject Prefixes

Affirmative copulative phrases are formed by prefixing the affixes of the first (I) and second (II) persons (subject prefixes) to substantive phrases and, when the SP is locative adverbial, those of the third (III) persons as well.[1]

e.g.
ni-muLozi	(I am a Losi)	(Is)
u-mutu yaamusa	(you are a kind person)	(IIs)
lu-batu babansu	(we are black people)	(I pl)
mu-batu babamusa	(you are kind people)	(II pl)
u-teŋi fona foo	(he is at that same place)	(1)
ba-kwasishanjo kwanu	(they are at the wet-garden here)	(2)
u-kumulena	(he is with the chief)	(1)
ba-kuboSitali	(they are with the Sitalis)	(2)

The affirmative inflection is changed to the negative by prefixing /ha- ~ a-/ (not).

Copulatives Consisting of Subjectivally Inflected Relative Stems[2]

Relative stems are affirmatively inflected, by prefixing subject affixes of all persons and classes. These constructions are a principal inflection of these stems which may act as predicates in substantival clauses. The stems are also inflected relatively and the resulting constructions are substantival.

e.g.
Sikuwa si-tata	(English is difficult)	(7)
Mutu yo u-musa	(This person is kind)	(1)
Batu bao ba-maswe	(These people are bad)	(2)
Lico li-munati	(The food is delicious)	(10)

---
[1] The subject prefixes are discussed on pp. 74-76.
[2] Relative stems are discussed and listed on pp. 31-34.

The affirmative inflection is changed to the negative by prefixing /ha- ~ a-/ (not).

ADVERBIAL PHRASES

Adverbial phrases inflected by /ka-/ (by means of)
SPs inflected by /ka-/ are adverbial instrumental in meaning. They also belong to the constituent class of adjuncts in verb phrases and indicate the means by which, or the material in reference to which, an action is done.

e.g. | | |
|---|---|
| Neninatilwe **ka-kota yetuna** | (I was beaten with a big stick) |
| Nenitile **ka-ngila ye** | (I came by this path) |
| Nenibulela **ka-taba yeo** | (I was speaking about that affair) |
| Nizamayile **ka-mota ye yesuna** | (I have travelled in this big car) |
| Neniutwile **ka-kaizoli yaka ka-liŋolo le** | (I heard about my sister by this letter) |
| Nifitile **ka-nako yabusihu** | (I arrived at night) |
| Neniutwile ku-kaizeli yaka **ka-liŋolo le** | (I heard from my sister by this letter) |
| Nenirutilwe **ka-likomu** ki-ndate | (I was taught about cattle by my father) |
| Una ashwile **ka-puso** yaLewanika | (He died in the reign of Lewanika) |
| ubulezi **ka-zamasimu** | (He spoke about gardening affairs) |
| Batile **ka-bubeli** | (They came two by two) |

Adverbial phrases inflected by /ni-/ (with)
(a) SPs inflected by /ni-/ are adverbial associative in meaning. They also belong to the constituent class of adjunct in verb phrases and indicate the

persons or things associated with the action.

e.g. *Una apila **ni-bana bahae*** (He was living with his children)
*Utile **ni-babaŋwi batu*** (He came with some other people)
*Zamaya **ni-puli yani*** (Go with that goat yonder)
*Nitile **ni-batu bali baŋwi*** (I came with the same people)

(b) They are frequently used in reciprocal extended verb phrases

e.g. *Balatana **ni-muenyi*** (He and the stranger love each other; lit. They love each other with the stranger)
*Nizibana **ni-mutu yo*** (I and this person know one another)

(c) Associative phrases are used after the verb /-na/ (be with) only in affirmative inflections.

e.g. *Nina ni-celete yeŋata* (I have a lot of money)
but *Hanina celete yeŋata* (I have not much money)
Note: *fakaufi ni-ndu* (near the house)
kwahule ni-ndu (far from the house)

Adverbials consisting of inflected stems

Adverbials of manner and degree are formed by prefixing /ha-/ to adjectival and relative stems as well as certain nouns.

e.g. *ha-ŋata* (often) cp. *-ŋata* (adjectival stem)
ha-munati (sweetly) *-munati* (relative stem)
ha-lishumi (ten times) *lishumi* (ten) (5)

POSSESSIVE PHRASES

SPs inflected by the possessive inflections are substantival constructions belonging, as secondary members, to the constituent classes of nuclear substantive and substantive in agreement in substantive phrases.

e.g.   *libizo la-mushimani yo*   (the name of this boy)   (5)

The possessive inflections are made up of a class affix and the morpheme /-a-/ of relationship. The class affix indicates the possessee or object of the relationship.

e.g.   *libizo **l-a-mushimani***   (the name it-of the boy)   (5)
       *piza **y-a-1izupa***   (a pot it-of clay)   (9)

The class affixes occur in the following forms.

	Singular		No number		Plural
1.	w-			2.	b-
3.	w-			4.	y-
5.	l-			6.	Ø-
7.	s-			8.	by-
9.	y-			10.	z-
11.	bw-				
12.	k-			13.	tw-
		14.	bw-		
		15.	kw-		
		16.	f-		
		17.	kw-		
		18.	mw-		

e.g.   *likomu za-mulena wapili wabuLozi*   (the cattle of the former   (10)
                                             chief of Lozi-land)
       buka ya-bubeli   (the second book)   (9)

Possessive inflections are used as constituents not only with SPs but also with pronominal stems and pronouns which refer to them. Possessive stems exist which refer to possessors of Is, IIs and class 1. Pronouns are used to indicate possessors of other persons and classes (see pp. 22-24.)

Is.	-ka
IIs.	-hau
III. 1	-hae

e.g.   *nja ya-ka*   (my dog)   (9)
       mukolo wa-hao   (your canoe)   (3)
       lipuli za-hae   (his cattle)   (10)
but   *bana ba-bona*   (their children)   (2)

Common possessive constructions are abbreviated.

e.g.   *muŋ' amunzi*   (owner of the village)   (1)
       mwan' aka   (my child)   (1)

Locatives based on SPs are possessive in classes 16 and 18; possessive and sometimes nominal in class 17.

e.g.   *fa-tafule yani*   (on that table)   (16) an inflected SP
cp.   *fatafule fani*   (**on** that table)   (16) an SP
e.g.   *mwa-ndu yani*   (in that house)   (18) an inflected SP
cp.   *mwandu mwani*   (**in** that house)   (18) an SP
e.g.   *kwa-likamba leo*   (at that shore)   (17) an inflected SP

cp.	*kwalikamba kolubata*	(to the river bank where	(17) an SP
	kuzamaya luna	we want to go)	
e.g.	*fa-pili yamota*	(in front of the car)	(16)
	kwa-mulaho wamota	(at the back of the car)	(17)
	mwa-hali yamota	(inside the car)	(18)

The noun prefix /**ku-**/ of class 17 forms complex nominal constructions when prefixed to phrases.

e.g.	*ku-mulena yena*	(the chief himself)	(17)
	Luzwile ku-zona zeo	(We have come from those over there)	(17)

SUBSTANTIVE CLAUSES

Constructional pattern:
+/- Subject + Predicate

The constituent class of subject includes every kind of substantive phrase or substantive. Its presence is optional in the clause whose nuclear element is the predicate. The class of predicates is made up of copulative phrases and copulatives.

The following are examples of affirmative inflected clauses:

e.g.	(a)	*Kelezo kimulyani*	(Advice is medicine)
		Museme woo kiwomunde hahulu	(That mat is a very good one)
		Munna yani kibondate	(That man is my father)
		Musebesi wakuluta kiwomunde	(The work of teaching is a good one)

(b)	*Mwan'aka ukwamunzi wamulena*	(My child is at the chief's village)
	Musal'ahau ukae?	(Where is your wife?)
(c)	*Pilu yahae itata cwale kalicwe*	(His heart is as hard as a stone)
	Munna yani umusa	(That man is kind)
	Kuzwapaula batu kumaswe	(To despise people is bad)

The following are examples of negative inflected clauses.

e.g.	(a)	*Batu ba hasi babatuna*	(These people are not strong ones)
		Museme woo hasi womunde	(That mat is not a good one)
	(b)	*Mwan'aka ha-a-kwamunzi*	(My child is not at the village)
	(c)	*Lico ze ha-li-munati*	(This food is not nice)

SUBSTANTIVAL SENTENCES

Substantival sentences consist of a substantival clause which may be accompanied by participial verbal clauses.

e.g.	*Niha aipahamisa hakankana, kimutu fela*	(Although he prides himself a great deal, he is only a commoner)
	Ha alila, kimwan'aka	(If he is crying, it is my child)
	Ha ahalifile, kikuli bamuhalifisize hape nihape	(If he is angry it is because they have given him cause for anger time and again)

Chapter 2

VERBAL CONSTRUCTIONS

The Verb Radical

The constructions of the verbal hierarchy are based on the verb radical as nuclear element.

e.g.   *-lat-*   (love, want)

The verb radical, of course, never appears by itself, but always in an inflected form. The simplest inflection of a verb radical is that of the imperative which consists of the terminal vowel /-a/ and an associated tone pattern (not marked here). The infinitive inflection /ku-...-a/ is also a simple one.

e.g.   *lat-a!*   (love)
       ku-lat-a   (to love, loving)

Another inflection is that of the negative principal present.

e.g.   *Ani-lat-i*   (I don't love)

The verb radical is the nuclear element in all of these examples. They show that the terminal vowels /-a/ and /-i/ are part of the inflection imposed on the verb radical and are distinct as morphemes from it. Verb radicals are phonologically incomplete since they lack a final vowel. This is always supplied by the inflection.

Simplex and Complex Verb Radicals

Verb radicals may be simplex or complex. Simplex radicals consist of a single morpheme.

e.g.   *-lat-*   (love)
       -lek-   (buy)

-zib- (know)
-lil- (cry)

Complex radicals are **constructions** consisting of simplex radicals + extensions or verbalisers. Simplex radicals + extensions are called **extended radicals.** Extensions are affix morphemes which extend the relations of the verb radical to complements and adjuncts in the verb phrase in ways beyond the power of the simplex radical.

e.g. *-zib-an-* (know one another) viz. */-zib/* (know) + */-an-/* the reciprocal extension

-fel-iz- (finish) viz. */-fel-/* (come to an end) + */-iz-/* the causative extension

-utw-isis- (hear well, understand) viz. */-utw-/* (hear) + */-isis-/* the intensive extension.

Simplex radicals with verbalisers are called **derived verb radicals.** Verbalisers are affix morphemes whereby verb radicals are formed from non-verbal stems such as nouns and ideophones.

e.g. *-hali-f-* (be angry) cp. */hali/* (anger) (9) + verbaliser */-f-/*.

-yuku-l- (paddle fast) cp. */yuku/* (paddling fast), an ideophone + verbaliser */-l-/*.

Both extended and derived verb radicals are constructions and occupy the first level of the verbal constructions.

The Verb Phrase

The second level of the verbal constructions is that of the verb phrase. It consists, in its fullest form, of verb radicals, both simplex and complex, together with their complements, both objects and adverbs, and with adjuncts which are normally adverbial. In verb phrases only the nuclear constituent of the verb radical is compulsory, while the presence of the other constituents, namely the object prefix, the object and adverbial complements and the adjuncts is optional.

The constructional pattern of the verb phrase is therefore defined as:
/+/- object prefix + verb radical +/- complements +/- adjuncts/

e.g. *-lat- nja* (want a dog) - verb radical + object complement
-lek- nama (buy meat) - verb radical + object complement
-yukul- mukolo (paddle canoe fast) - derived verb radical + object complement
-pil– nibana bahae (live with his children) - verb radical + adjunct
-bin– hamunati (sing sweetly) - verb radical + adverbial complement
-latan– nimuenyi (love and be loved by a stranger) - extended verb radical + adjunct
-mu-halifizis- (give him cause for anger) - object prefix + extended verb radical
-i-pahamis- (pride oneself) - reflexive object prefix + extended verb radical

The Inflected Verb Phrase

The third level of the verbal hierarchy of constructions is that of the inflected verb phrase. The constituents of the verb phrase are (1) the inflection, and (2) the verb phrase. Both constituents are compulsory.

Thus the constructional pattern of the inflected verb phrase is:

/+ inflection + verb phrase/.

The inflection consists of combinations of inflecting affix morphemes indicating affirmation or negation, the subject, the tense, the mode and so on.

e.g. *Ni-lek-a nama* (I am buying meat) - the subject prefix /*ni-*/ (I) and the terminal vowel /*-a*/ constitute the inflection.

A-ni-lat-i nja (I don't want a dog) - the negative prefix /*a-*/, the subject prefix *ni-* and the terminal vowel /*-i*/ constitute the inflection.

Ba-muhalifisiz-e (They gave him cause for anger) - the subject prefix /*ba-*/ (they) and the terminal vowel /*-e*/ constitute the inflection.

Verbal Clause

The fourth level of the verbal constructions is that of the verbal clause. This consists of a subject and predicate. The predicate of verbal clauses is an inflected verb phrase.

e.g. *Nna nileka nama* (As for me, I am buying meat)
Batho bao bayukula mukolo (Those people are paddling the canoe fast)

In the clause the subject is usually a substantive or substantive phrase and is an optional constituent.

Verbal Sentence

A fifth level of the verbal constructions is that of the verbal sentence. In a verbal sentence there is a principal clause which is verbal accompanied by one or more clauses, either principal or subordinate.

e.g. *Nihaiba mezi abubela kwamulaho* (Although the river is running
kamata, batu bao bayukula mukolo strongly against them, those people

	are paddling the canoe fast)
Kakuli bomma bakula kacenu,	(Because my mother is sick today,
nileka nama	I am buying meat)

The above then are the levels of verbal constructions. The most complex unit is the **sentence** (level V). Its constituents are **clauses** (level IV). The constituents of the clause are subject and predicate, **an inflected verb phrase** (level III). The constituents of the inflected verb phrase are the verbal inflections and the **verb phrase** (level II). The **verb radical** (level I) is the nuclear constituent of the verb phrase.

THE VERB RADICAL

Radicals may be **simplex, adoptive, derived, extended** or **re-duplicated.**

Simplex radicals

These consist of a single morpheme,

e.g. *-hul-* (grow) cp. *ku-hul-a* (to grow)
-lim- (cultivate) cp. *ku-lim-a* (to cultivate)

Commonly simplex radicals consist phonologically of consonant-vowel-consonant (CVC) but examples of radicals which are phonologically CV, VC, CC, C, CVCVC and other patterns are found.

e.g. CV : *-lu-* (own) cp. *ku-lu-a* (to own)
VC : *-ez-* (make) cp. ku-ez-a (to make)
CC : *-ns-* (take out) cp. *ku-ns-a* (to take out)
C : *-f-* (give) cp. *ku-f-a* (to give)
CVCVC : *-sebez-* (work) cp. *ku-sebez-a* (to work)

Adoptive radicals

SiLozi has a number of verb radicals which it has adopted from other languages, in the main from English and Afrikaans. In being adopted the radicals are made to conform to siLozi phonology and morphology. Thus they normally end in a consonant and are inflected in the same way as original siLozi radicals.

e.g.   *ku-tolok-a*   (to interpret)   cp.   *tolk*   (interpret)   Afrikaans
       ku-temp-a   (to stamp)   cp.   *stamp*   English
       ku-cay-a   (to hit)   cp.   *-tshay-* (hit)   Ndebele

Like simplex radicals, adoptive radicals are morphologically simple, they are not constructions.

Derived radicals

Derived radicals are constructions in which the first constituent is either an ideophone or a substantival stem. The second constituent is a verbaliser, (i.e. the element which is suffixed to substantival stems and ideophones to form verb radicals). Derived radicals are nuclear constituents in verb phrases.

Radicals derived from ideophones. There is a large class of derived verb radicals whose constituents are **ideophone** and, **verbaliser.** Common verbalisers in such constructions are: /-k-/, /-l-/, /-m-/, /-n-/, /-ny-/, /-t-/, /-z-/.

e.g.   *-yuku-k-*   (go fast, of a canoe) cp. *yuku*   (moving fast, of a canoe)
       -yuku-l-   (paddle canoe fast)   cp. *yuku*   (ditto)
       -luku-m-   (throb)   cp. *luku*   (jumping)
       -fumya-n-   (stink)   cp. *fumya*   (stinking)
       -ziki-ny-   (wobble, shake)   cp. *ziki-ziki*   (shaking)
       -puku-t-   (use bellows)   cp. *puku-puku* (blowing)

-caculu-z- (multiply) cp. *caculu* (growing)

Radicals derived from substantive stems. There is a small class of derived verb radicals whose constituents are a stem (either nominal, adjectival or relative) and a verbaliser. Common verbalisers in such constructions are: /-f-/, /-fal-/, /-faz-/, /-b-/.

e.g.	*-hali-f-*	(become angry)	cp. *buhali*	(anger)	(14)
	-sweu-fal-	(become white)	cp. *-sweu*	(white)	(adj.)
	-tata-fal-	(become difficult)	cp. *-tata*	(hard)	(rel.)
	-nolo-faz-	(soften)	cp. *bunolo*	(softness)	(14)
	-mai-b-	(become unlucky)	cp. *bumai*	(bad luck)	(14)

Extended radicals

Extended radicals are constructions in which the first constituent is a verb radical, which may be simplex, adoptive or derived. The second constituent is an extension or combination of extensions. Extensions modify the basic significance of the radicals which they extend in various ways. One result of this is to affect the kind of verb phrase of which they may be the nuclear constituent. The ability to command and appear with object complements possible to a simplex radical may be (i) **reinforced**, (ii) **restricted** or (iii) **widened** by the addition of an extension.

e.g. the verb phrase /-lob- piza/ (break a pot) is **reinforced** by the extensive extension /-ak-/,

viz. *-lob-ak- piza* (break a pot to pieces)

It is **restricted** by the neuter extension /-eh-/,

viz. *-lob-eh- (piza)* (get broken (of a pot))

The former complement of the unextended radical may now be used with the neuter extended radical only as subject.

e.g.   *Piza i-lob-eh-ile*   (The pot has got broken)

It is **widened** by the applied extension /-el-/, with the result that another complement is required.

viz.   *-lob-el- piza mukwenyani*   (break a pot for, i.e. to spite, a mother-in-law)

According to this threefold effect of extensions on the collocational relationships of verb radicals and verb phrases, they are divided into three classes:

(a) extensions which do not disturb such relationships;

(b) extensions which restrict such relationships; and

(c) extensions which set these relationships in a wider context.

a) Verbal extensions which do not disturb the collocational relationships of verb radicals and verb phrases,

(1)   /-ak-/ (extensive, repeated action)

e.g.   *-buz-ak-*   (ask many questions)   cp. *-buz-*   (ask)
       -lob-ak-   (break into pieces)   cp. *-lob-*   (break)
       -nat-ak-   (beat again and again)   cp. *-nat-*   (beat)
       -tab-ak-   (wound in different places) cp. *-tab-*   (wound)

(2) /-ang-/ (frequent, habitual action)

e.g.   *-bof-ang-*   (tether daily)   cp. *-bof-*   (bind)
       -utw-ang-   (hear often)   cp. *-utw-*   (hear)
       -tahw-ang- (get drunk often)   cp. *-tahw-*   (get drunk)

(3) /-isis-/ (Intensive: thorough, effective action)

e.g. *-utw-isis-* (understand thoroughly)   cp. *-utw-* (hear)
      -zib-isis- (know very well)   cp. *-zib-* (know)
      -buz-isis- (cross-question)   cp. *-buz-* (ask)

(4) /*-elel-*/ ~ /*-elez-*/ (Perfective: action carried through to completion)

e.g. *-y-elel-*   (go for good)   cp. *-y-*   (go)
      -om-elel-   (dry up)   cp. *-om-*   (dry)
      -fit-elel- (pass right through)   cp. *-fit-* (pass by)

This extension takes the form /*-elez-*/ after radicals ending in /c, j, ny, s, sh, z, zw/ i.e. alveolar or palatal stops, spirants and nasals.

e.g. *-biz-elez-* (call all)

b) Verbal extensions which restrict the collocational relationships of verb radicals and verb phrases,

(5) /*-an-*/ (Associative: action or state affecting parts of a whole in common)

e.g. *-lamb-an-*   (be well kneaded as a lump)
      -fulum-an- (be upside down)
      -limb-an-   (crowd together)   cp. *-limb-* (press down)

(6) (i) /*-al-*/ (Neuter: action easily performed, action done without reference
    (ii) /*-eh-*/ to agent, perhaps becoming a state)

e.g. *-bon-al-*   (be visible)   cp. *-bon-* (see)
      -utw-al-   (be audible)   cp. *-utw-* (hear)
      -si-al-   (be left)   cp. *-si-*   (leave)
      -lat-eh-   (get lost)   cp. *-lat-* (throw away)
      -ez-eh-   (be feasible)   cp. *-es-*   (do)

	-sab-eh-	(be dreadful)	cp. *-sab-*	(fear)

(7) /-w-/ ~ /-iw-/ (Passive: action undergone by a subject, often as the result of some agency)

e.g.	*-zib-w-*	(be known)	cp. *-zib-*	(know)
	-buz-w-	(be asked)	cp. *-buz-*	(ask)
	-lob-w-	(be broken)	cp. *-lob-*	(break)
	-zamay-w-	(be walked)	cp. *-zamay-*	(walk)

The form /-iw-/ is used after radicals which are of C, CC, CV phonological shape, also radicals ending in /-Cw[1]-/ and as an alternative in other cases to /-w-/.

e.g.	*-f-iw-*	(be given)	cp. *-f-*	(give)
	-ns-iw-	(be taken out)	cp. *-ns-*	(take out)
	-si-iw-	(be left)	cp. *-si-*	(leave)
	-utw-iw-	(be heard)	cp. *-utw-*	(hear)
	-zib-iw-	(be known)	cp. *-zib-*	(know)

(8) /-an-/ (Reciprocal action)

e.g.	*-zib-an-*	(know one another)	cp. *-zib-*	(know)
	-bon-an-	(see each other)	cp. *-bon-*	(see)
	-utw-an-	(hear each other)	cp. *-utw-*	(hear)
	-lat-an-	(love one another)	cp. *-lat-*	(love)

c) Verbal extensions which set the relationship of verb radicals and verb phrases in a wider context

---

[1] i.e. consonant + w

(9) /-el-/ ~ /-en-/ ~ /-ez-/ (Applied: action done on behalf of or to the detriment of someone; towards or with respect to some person, thing or place)

e.g. -lek-el-   (buy for)   cp. -lek-   (buy)
      -halif-el- (be angry with)   cp. -halif- (be angry)
      -c-el-   (eat out of, for) cp. -c-   (eat)

The form /-en-/ is used after a few radicals ending in /m, n/ and that of /-ez-/ after radicals ending in the alveolar spirants /s, z, zw/ and the palatals /c, j, ny, sh/ (Gowlett, 1967, p. 39, 41).

e.g. -yendam-en- (lean against) cp. -yendam- (lean)
      -biz-ez-   (call to, for) cp. -biz-   (call)
      -fos-ez-   (do wrong to)   cp. -fos-   (do wrong)

(10) (i) /-Y-/ (Causative: action brought about by the action of an agent on a person or thing)

This extension is given the conventional form of /-Y-/ to indicate that it does not occur as such but is manifested only in a restricted number of morphophonemic changes. These occur in radicals as follows:

Final radical consonant h + Y > s
                         k + Y > s
                         l + Y > z
                         n + Y > ny

e.g. -tus-   (take away) cp. -tuh-   (go away)
      -hupuz- (remind)   cp. -hupul- (remember)
      -keny- (insert)   cp. -ken-   (enter)

(ii) /-is-/ (Causative: action brought about by the action of an agent on a person or thing, in some cases assisting the action to take place).

e.g.	-lobal-is-	(cause to sleep, sleep with)	cp.	-lobal-	(sleep)
cp.	-lobaz-	(put to bed)			
	-fuluh-is-	(help to paddle)	cp.	-fuluh-	(peddle)
	-zub-is-	(offer tobacco to)	cp.	-zub-	(smoke)
	-bal-is-	(teach to read)	cp.	-bal-	(read)
	-fol-is-	(wait till sunset)	cp.	-fol-	(get cool)

Combinations of Extensions

Radicals and verb phrases are extended not only by single extensions but by certain combinations of extensions. Common combinations of extensions are the following:

10 + 2	-is-ang-	e.g.	-bon-is-ang-	(show often)
8 + 9	-an-el-		-bon-an-el-	(see each other for)
9 + 8	-el-an-		-lek-el-an-	(buy for each other)
5 + 9	-an-elel-		-long-an-elel-	(all embark) cp. -long- (load)
6 + 2	-eh-ang-		-lob-eh-ang-	(get broken often)
10 + 7	-is-w-		-bon-is-w-	(be shown)
9 + 7	-el-w-		-ŋol-el-w-	(have written for one)
6 + 9 + 7	-eh-el-w-		-siny-eh-el-w-	(have spoilt for one)

Reduplicated Radicals

Verb radicals may be reduplicated and form a construction at Level I, the level of the radical. The constituents are two identical radicals save in the case of a radical of C or CVC+ shape. In the case of C radicals the reduplicated radical is preceded by a stabiliser /a/.

e.g.	-c-ac-	(eat a little)	-c-	(eat)

    -nw-a-nw-   (drink a little)   *-nw-*   (drink)

In the case of CVC+ radicals there is either complete reduplication or, less commonly, reduplication only of the first CVC of the radical (Gowlett, p. 84-5)

e.g. *-honon-honon-* (keep on grumbling) *-honon-* (grumble)
     -kopa-kopan-   (keep on meeting)   *-kopan-* (meet)
     -buz-buz-   (keep on asking)   *-buz-*   (ask)

Repetition of radicals may imply repetition, as in the above examples. It may imply half-hearted, haphazard action done here and there, now and then,

e.g. *-tom-tom-* (plant here and there) *-tom-* (plant)

or an action done for a short time,

e.g. *-pang-pang-* (build for a while, incompletely)

or an action occurring to a limited extent,

e.g. *-shend-shend-* (rebuke gently)
     -ekez-ekez-   (increase a little now and then)

THE VERB PHRASE

The verb radical as discussed on pages 51-59 is the nuclear constituent of the construction at the next level in the hierarchy of verbal constructions, namely the verb phrase.

The verb phrase, besides the verb radical, may contain the following optional constituents:
    (i)   an object prefix;
    (ii) an object complement or complements;

(iii) an adverbial complement or complements;
(iv) an adjunct or adjuncts.

e.g. *-bup-* (mould), a verb radical, in the inflected verb phrase
Ba-bup-a (They mould)

-li-bup- (mould them), object prefix + verb radical, in the inflected verb phrase
Ba-li-bup-a (They mould them)

-li-bup- lipizana (mould the pots), object prefix, radical and object complement, in the inflected verb phrase
Ba-li-bup-a lipizana (They mould the pots)

-li-bup- lipizana kwanuka (mould the pots at the river), object prefix, radical, object complement and adverbial complement, in the inflected verb phrase
Ba-li-bup-a lipizana kwanuka (They mould the pots at the river)

-li-bup- lipizana kwanuka kamazoho (mould the pots at the river by hand), object prefix, radical, object complement, adverbial complement and adjunct, in the inflected verb phrase.
Ba-li-bup-a lipizana kwanuka kamazoho (They mould the pots by hand at the river)

It is the verb phrase (VP) with all its internal relationships which is inflected, not just the verb radical. To recognise the existence of the VP as a constant constituent at the level of the inflected VP, compare the following, differently inflected, VPs.

e.g. *Ku-li-bup-a lipizana kwanuka kamazoho*
(To mould the pots by hand at the river) (infinitive)
Li-bup-e lipizana kwanuka kamazoho
(Mould the pots by hand at the river) (imperative)
N-a-li-bup-a lipizana kwanuka kamazoho
(I mould the pots by hand at the river) (Affirmative principal present)
Ha-ni-li-bup-i lipizana kwanuka kamazoho
(I do not mould the pots by hand at the river) (Negative principal present)

It is this unit and its internal relationships which are studied in this section.[1]

THE STRUCTURE OF THE VP

The VP is characterised by the optional constituents, viz. the object prefix, the complements and the adjuncts and the relationships which obtain between them and the radical, the compulsory constituent. The constituents are termed optional in that a VP and an inflected VP may exist without them. All the following are inflected VPs with identical inflection, viz. /Ni-a...a/ (affirmative principal present).

viz. *Ni-a-**li-bup**-a*   (I mould them)

*N-a-**li-bup**-a lipizana*   (I mould the pots)

*N-a-**li-bup**-a kamazoho* (I mould them by hand)

---
[1] In this section, VPs are in bold in examples.

N-a-li-bup-a kwanuka   (I mould them at the river)

The VP is a construction which shows enormous variety in its possible realisations. In order to describe this variety and, at the same time, the underlying structure, each of the constituents must be examined in turn. They will be described in this order:

(a) the adjuncts

(b) the complements

(c) the object prefixes

a) The Adjuncts

The term adjunct indicates a constituent class which includes both constructions and particles.

(a) The constructions consist of adverbial phrases and adverbials. The adverbial phrases are substantive phrases inflected by the adverbial affixes /*ki-*/ (of agency), /*ka-*/ (of instrumentality), /*ni-*/ (of association), /*sina-*/ (of manner) and /*-ŋi*/ (locative). Adverbials are substantives (potential substantive phrases) inflected by these affixes and inflected stems inflected by the affix /*ha-*/ (of manner).

(i)   /*ki-*/ (agency). Adverbial phrases and adverbials inflected by /*ki-*/

commonly occur in a passive extended VP.

e.g.	*-cis-w- kilizazi*	(be burnt by the sun)
cp.	*Mabele aka-cisw-a kilizazi*	(the corn may/will be burnt by the sun)
e.g.	*-kataz-w- kisitukutuku*	(be tired by the heat)
cp.	*lu-katazw-a kisitukutuku*	(we are exhausted by the heat)
e.g.	*U-bulailw-e kitau yetuna*	(He was killed by a big lion)
e.g.	*U-bulailw-e kibutuku bobumaswe*	(He was killed by a serious disease)
e.g.	*U-bonw-i kisikwala seo*	(He was seen by that artisan)
e.g.	*U-bonw-i kibanna babona*	(He was seen by their husbands)

(ii) /ka-/ (instrumentality). A number of relationships are conveyed by this inflecting affix.

e.g.	*-lim- kamihuma*	(cultivate with hoes)
	-bulay- kamalumo amaŋata	(kill with many spears)
	-i-tol- kalisuka	(anoint self with red ochre)
	-bes- litina kamulilo	(bake bricks with fire)
	-tah- kasilimo sa1970	(come in the year 1970)
	-tah- kanako yabusihu	(come at night-time)
	-ez- katata	(do with difficulty)
	-ez- kabunolo	(do gently)
	-ez- kabaka laŋi?	(do for what reason?)
	-ez- kazazi lapili	(do on Monday)
	-ez- kazazi nizazi	(do every day, lit. by day and day)
	-ez- kanako ninako	(do regularly, by time and time)
	-zamay- kabubeli	(walk in twos)

(iii) /*ni-*/ (association)

e.g. *-tah- nibanna babona*   (come with their husbands)

  -y- niluna   (go with us)

Adverbials of this kind are common after the verb radicals /*-na*/ (be with) /*-ba*/ (be) in the affirmative but not in the negative.

e.g. *Ni-na ni-celete*   (I have money)
cp.   *Hani-na celete*   (I have no money)
e.g. *Ne-ni-na ni-celete*   (I had some money)
cp.   *Ne-nisi-na celete*   (I had no money)
e.g. *Nita-ba ni-celete*   (I will have some money)
cp.   *Nita-be nisi-na celete*   (I will have no money)
e.g. *Nihaiba ni-na ni-celete...* (Although I have money...)
cp.   *Nihaiba nisi-na celete...* (Although I have no money...)
  -na nimezi amaŋata mwasibaka se (be with much water in this area)
  -na nibusunso bobulikani   (be with enough relish)

(iv) /*sina-*/ (like)

e.g. *-om- sina mushabati*   (be dry as sand)

(v)   /*-ŋi*/ (locative). This locative inflecting affix, active in the other Sotho languages, survives in inflected possessive phrases like:

  (si)bakeŋi samasimu   (instead of the gardens, with regard to the gardens)

  bakeŋi sakutaha   (instead of coming)

e.g. *-lat- kusebeza bakeŋi sakuitulela* (like to work instead of resting)

(vi) /**ha-**/ (manner, degree). This affix is prefixed to adjectival and relative stems to form adverbials of manner.

e.g.
-lat- hahulu	(love greatly)
-tah- haŋata	(come often)
-zib- naha hande hahulu	(know the country very well)
hakae?	(how many times?)
haŋwi	(once)

(vii) Note the following constructions which appear to incorporate demonstratives and interrogative stems:

cwale (like this), **cwalo** (like that), **cwana** (thus), **cwaŋi?** (how?) **cwanuŋu** (now). The form **cwale** is often used with adverbials inflected by /ka-/,

e.g.
cwale kafulaulo	(like flour)
cwale kalicwe	(like a stone)

(b) No examples of particles have been noted.

b) The Complements

Complements differ from adjuncts in being substantives or substantive phrases, whereas adjuncts are inflected substantive phrases, inflected substantives or inflected stems, the inflecting affixes not being class affixes.

(a) Adverbial complements

Complements differ from one another in class, in meaning and in the range of radicals with which they appear. The following types of complement can appear with the widest range of radicals. Like the adjuncts they are adverbial in meaning and define that of the radical in terms of place, time, degree and manner.

(i) **Adverbial complements of place.** These are phrases of classes 16, 17 and 18. Those of classes 16 and 18 are mainly possessive, those of class 17 mainly nominal and possessive. Nouns of other classes are used locatively as well.

Cl. 16	:	*-pil- falinaha*	(lit. survive on finger nails, viz. have a narrow escape)
		-in- famuseme	(sit on a mat)
		-fit- falikamba	(arrive at the shore)
		-be- fatafule	(place on the table)
		-fit- fapili yahae	(arrive ahead of him)
		-fit- fakaufi nikota	(near the tree)
		-fit- fani	(there)
Cl. 17	:	*-fit- kumulena*	(arrive at the chief)
		-fit- kusili	(arrive at another place)
		-fit- kwamulaho	(arrive behind)
		-fit- kwamushitu	(arrive at the forest)
		-fit- kwakota	(arrive at the tree)
		-fit- kwateŋi	(arrive there)
		-fit- kwaSenanga	(arrive at Senanga)
		-fit- kwapili	(arrive in front)
		-fit- kwahule nikota	(arrive far from the tree)
		-fit- kokuŋwi	(arrive elsewhere)
		-fit- kwani	(arrive over there)

Cl. 18 : *-pil- mwandu*   (live in the house)
          -w- mwanuka   (fall into the river)
          -be- mwatasi   (place underneath)
          -be- mwani   (place in there)

Adverbial complements of place do not indicate motion either to or from. These notions, as well as that of rest, are conveyed by the radical with which the complements occur. Phrases inflected by /*fa-*/, /*mwa-*/ and /*kwa-*/ indicate places which are respectively relatively near and within sight, relatively near but out of sight, and far.

cp.   *Ba-yah-ile falilundu*   (They live on the hill, not far, in sight)
       Ba-yah-ile mwalilundu   (They live on the hill, not far, but out of sight)
       Ba-yah-ile kwalilundu   (They live far away on the hill)

Other classes:
    mambala   (far)   (6)
    mabapa   (opposite)   (6)
    njongo-njongo   (high up)   (9)

(ii) **Adverbial complements of time.** These are phrases and substantives of classes 16, 17, 18, 6 and other classes,

-fit-kwamulaho   (arrive afterwards)
-shw- mwamusipili   (die during a journey)
-shw- kwamakalelo akweli (die at the beginning of the month)
mabane   (yesterday)   (6)

musihali omutuna	(high noon)	(3)
musihali wakakusasa	(morning)	(3)
musihali wamanzibwana	(afternoon)	(3)

(iii) **Adverbial complements of manner.** These are certain substantive phrases and substantives of class 7 and other classes.

e.g.
-tib- sindondo	(drown like a pitcher sinking)	(7)
-mat- sikusha	(run together)	(7)
-ez- maswe	(do badly)	(6)
-fez- mutumbi	(finish completely)	(3)

(b) Object Complements

Object complements consist of substantive phrases or substantives. Verb radicals differ widely in the number and type of object complements with which they may occur. Some radicals occur with object complements which may be accompanied by object prefixes or be such that object prefixes may be substituted for them. These are called **primary object complements**. Others occur only with **secondary object complements** which are those incapable of governing an object prefix either as a co-referent or referent. Still other radicals do not occur with object complements.

e.g. Radical with primary object complements.

-nat- nja katupa   (hit a dog with a stick)

Radical with secondary object complement

-holofal- liito   (get hurt (in) the eye)

Radical with no object complement

-katal-   (become tired)

-tuk-   (blaze, of a fire)

Examples of VPs with object complements:

>*Linyunywani li-**tus**-a **batu*** (Birds help people)
>*Bana haba-**zum**-i **lifolofolo zetuna*** (Children do not hunt big game)
>***Mwamisipili yaka** ni-**bon**-i **zeŋata*** (In my travels I have seen many things)

Object complements may be compound when joined by /ni-/,

e.g. ***-bat- nama ni-bucwala*** (want meat and beer)
>*Bana ba-**lat**-a **kuopela ni-kubapala*** (Children like to sing and play)
>*Uka-**bon**-a **kuli ulobezi ni-kuli ulola fela*** (You can see that he is sleeping and that he is only dreaming)

c) The Object Prefixes

The last constituent in the VP is the object prefix. The place of the object prefix in a VP is always immediately in front of the radical

e.g. *Mu-**bon**-a **nuka** na?* (Do you see the river?)
>*Lw-a- **i-bon**-a* (We see it)

The object prefixes for the first, second and third persons, and all classes are as follows:

		Singular	No number		Plural
I		ni-			lu-
II		ku-			mi-
III	1	mu-		2.	ba-

	Singular	No number		Plural
3.	u-		4.	i-
5.	li-		6.	a-
7.	si-		8.	bi-
9.	i-		10.	zi-
11.	lu-			
12.	ka-		13.	tu-
		14. bu-		
		15. ku-		
		17. ku-		

An object prefix may be either a referent (in the absence of a substantive in the VP) or a co-referent (when the substantive is present in the VP to which it refers). In either case there is agreement between object prefixes and substantives.

Object prefixes as referents

    *Na u-**lat**-a **libala**?*   (Do you like the plain?)
    *Hani-**li-lat**-i*   (I don't like it)
    *Ni-**mu-zib**-ile*   (I knew him)
    *Na mushimani waka u-**ku-tus**-ize?*   (Has my boy helped you?)

Object prefixes as co-referents

    ***Bona buhobe** ba-**bu-kup**-a kumulena*   (As for the bread, they ask for it from the chief)
    *Muta-**u-bon**-a munzi wabona*   (You will see it, their village, that is)
    *Ba-**bi-ng**-ile **bicacani***   (They have taken the shrubs)

The reflexive prefix /i-/, referring back to the subject of the VP, but as object, also occurs immediately in front of the radical. The combination of /i-/ + radical causes morphophonemic changes to the radical similar to those involved in the combination: noun prefix /N-/ of class 9 + noun stem. That is, the initial phone (i.e. sound) of the radical is changed in many instances where the following sequences occur:

/i-/ + initial /b/ > /p/ e.g. -i-pus- (rule oneself) cp. -bus- (rule)
/f/ > /p/ e.g. -i-p- (give oneself) cp. -f- (give)
/l/ > /t/ e.g. -i-tat- (love oneself) cp. -lat- (love)
/y/ > /c/ e.g. -i-cahel- (build for oneself) cp. -yahel- (build for)
/h/ > /k/ e.g. i-kolofaz- (hurt oneself) cp. -holofaz- (hurt)
/w/ > /kw/ e.g. -i-kwis- (trip oneself) cp. -wis- (cause to fall)
/Ø/ > /k/ e.g. -i-kabel- (apportion to oneself) cp. -abel- (share out)

No examples of the object prefix and the reflexive prefix occurring together were acceptable to informants.

THE INFLECTED VERB PHRASE

The inflected verb phrase is the verbal construction at the third level of construction. Its constructional pattern is as follows:
Inflection + VP

The structure of the VP has already been treated on pages 61-71. The present section is concerned with the constituent classes of inflecting morphemes and the system whereby members of these constituent classes are combined into inflections.[1]

CATEGORIES OF INFLECTION

Finite and Non-Finite Inflections
Finite inflections include a subject prefix; non-finite inflections do not. The latter include the infinitive and imperative inflections,

e.g.   *ku-bes-a nama*   (to roast meat)
       Bes-a nama!   (Roast meat!)

Primary and Secondary Finite Inflections
Finite inflections may be divided into two classes, **primary** and **secondary**. In primary inflections there is reference to **time**, conveyed by tense signs. Primary inflections have three corresponding forms,

(i)   **principal**, used for the predicates of main clauses;

e.g.   *Munna w-a-lwan-a*   (The man fights)

(ii) **participial**, used for the predicates of subordinate clauses;

e.g.   *Ha munna a-lwan-a...*   (If the man fights...)

(iii) **relative**, used for predicates which are secondary members of the constituent classes of substantive in SPs.

e.g.   *Munna ya-lwan-a*   (A man who fights). See pp. 31-34

[1.] In the following section the inflection in examples is in bold to distinguish it from the VP which is inflected.

Secondary inflections also have three corresponding forms,

(i) **hortative;**

e.g. *Ha-a-lwan-e* (Let him fight)

(ii) **"present" subjunctive;**

e.g. *(kuli) a-lwan-e* ((so that) he should fight)

(iii) **"past" subjunctive** or consecutive.

e.g. *(kufitela) a-lwan-a* ((until) he fought)

Secondary inflections do not of themselves refer to time. The "present" subjunctive occurs in subordinate or consecutive clauses in sentences where present or future tenses have been used while the "past" subjunctive occurs in consecutive clauses where the past or potential tenses have been used.

These six inflections, three primary and three secondary, are sometimes referred to as moods or modal forms.

Affirmative and negative inflections. Inflections are affirmative unless they are marked by a negative morpheme. This is the prefix /*ha-* ~ *a-*/ in the case of principal inflections and /*-si-* ~ *-sa-*/ in the case of others. In general there is a corresponding negative inflection for every affirmative one.

Inflecting Morphemes of VPs

The inflecting morphemes exist in classes from which members are drawn and combine in a regular order. The following classes of inflecting morphemes can be distinguished: prefixal morphemes, subject prefixes, negative signs, tense signs, aspect signs and terminals.

Prefixal Morphemes

In finite inflections the subject prefix is the first constituent except in the negative principal and hortative. In these inflections, prefixal morphemes precede the subject prefix,

e.g. (a) the negative prefix /ha- ~ a-/
      (b) the hortative prefix /ha- ~ a-/

e.g. ***Ha-ni**-lwan-i*   (I don't fight)
      ***Ha-lu**-bon-e*   (let us see)

Subject Prefixes

(a) In all finite inflections, one member of the constituent class of subject prefix (sp) appears as a constituent of the inflection. The function of the sp is to relate the predicate (inflected verb phrase) of a clause to its subject which, as an optional constituent of the clause, may either be present or merely referred to.

e.g. *Batu **ba**-bon-a mililo*   (The people see the fires)
cp.   ***Ba**-bon-a mililo*   (They see the fires)

(b) The relation of subject and predicate is one of **agreement** in person and number or class. Non-agreement is allowed and indeed, preferred, where a noun subject other than of classes 1, 2, 1a and 2a indicates a person or persons. In this case, the subject prefix of the inflection is of classes 1 or 2 though the subject does not belong to those classes.

e.g. *Lisole **u**-lwan-a kalilumo*   (The soldier fights with spears)
cp.   *Liiba **li**-fuf-a kamoya*   (The dove flies through the air)

(c) There are two forms of the sps for the Ist and IInd persons and three for each class of the IIIrd person. The second of the two forms in each case is of C or CC shape and occurs before the tense signs consisting of the vowel /a/ (viz. the sign of the "long" present, and that of the past subjunctive). The third of the three forms in each case is used in relative inflections. As appears from inspection, the sps of series (iii) are complex and reflect an earlier construction consisting of a demonstrative, first position, and the subject prefix,

e.g.   *Liiba leli-fuf-a*   (a dove which flies)

In classes 1, 3, 4, 6 and 9 the vowels of the sps of series (iii) are long, reflecting the coalescence of two vowels at an earlier stage[1].

e.g.   yo:- < yo- + a-   (1)
       o:- < wo- + u-   (3)
       e:- < ye- + i-   (4)
       a:- < a- +a-   (6)
       e:- < ye- + i-   (9)

	(i)	(ii)	(iii)
I p. sing.	ni-	n-	
I p. plur.	lu-	lw-	
II p. sing.	u- ~ ku-	w-	
II p. plur.	mu	mw-	
III p. 1.	u- ~ a-	w- ~ Ø-	ya- (ya:-)
2.	ba-	b-	baba-
3.	u-	w-	o- (o:-)
4.	i-	y-	e- (e:-)

[1]. The colon /:/ inserted after a vowel indicates that it is a long vowel.

	5.	li-	l-		leli-
	6.	a-	Ø-		a- (a:-)
	7.	si-	s-		sesi-
	8.	bi-	by-		byebi-
	9.	i-	y-		e- (e:-)
	10.	li-	z-		ze- (ze:-)
	11.	lu-	lw-		lolu-
	12.	ka-	k-		kaka-
	13.	tu-	tw-		totu-
	14.	bu-	bw-		bobu-
	15.	ku-	kw-		koku-
	17.	ku	kw-		koku-

(d) **Alternate Forms** are:-

(i) The form /-**ku**-/ of the second person occurs after the hortative prefix,

e.g. *A-ku-ni-tus-e* (Please help me)

(ii) The forms /**u**-/ and /**w**-/ of class 1 are used in affirmative principal tenses except the potential. Otherwise the forms /a-/ and /Ø-/ are used.

e.g. *U-zib-a hande* (He knows well)
cp. *Ha-a-zib-i hande* (He does not know well)
e.g. *W-a-bu-lek-a, bucwala* (He is buying some, beer that is)
cp. *U-bu-lek-ile a-nw-a (Ø-a-nw-a)* (He bought some and drank)

Negative Signs

There are two negative prefixes /-*sa*-/ and /-*si*-/ in addition to the prefixal negative prefix /*ha*- ~ *a*-/.

(a) /-*sa*-/ occurs in the infinitive, participial present and past, relative present and past and the subjunctive.

e.g.
ku-sa-zib-a	(not to know)
niha ba-sa-zib-i	(although they do not know)
batu baba-sa-zib-i	(people who do not know)
ha mu-sa-bon-a	(if you did not see)
niha ba-sa-zib-a	(although they did not know)

(b) /*si*-/ occurs in the imperative, the principal, participal and relative past and potential/future, and the subjunctive.

e.g.
Si-zamay-i![1]	(Do not go)
Si zamay-e-ŋi	(Do not go! pl)
Ha-ni-si-ka-zib-a	(I did not know)
niha ni-si-ka-zib-a	(although I did not know)
batu baba-si-ka-zib-a	(people who did not know)
Ni-ka-si-halif-i	(I will/would not get angry)
alt. *Ni-ka-si-ke na-halif-a*	
niha ba-ka-si-halif-i	(although they will/would not get angry)
alt. *niha ba-si-ke ba-halif-a*	
Ni-si-utw-i mulumo	(I must not hear a sound)
alt. *Ni-si-ke na-utwa*	

Note that in the potential, where /-*ka*-/ occurs, the negative sign follows the tense sign. In the past, it precedes the tense sign.

---

[1] Some siLozi speakers prefer the negative subjunctives *U-sa-zamay-e!* (Do not go!), *Mu-sa-zamay-e!* (Do not go! – plural).

Tense Signs

(a) /-*a*-/ (/*a:*-/) : affirmative principal present, long form

e.g. *Munna w-a-lu-bon-a*   (The man sees us)

(b) /-*ta*-/ : affirmative future, principal, participal and relative

e.g. *U-ta-lek-a nama*   (she will buy meat)
      nihaiba ni-ta-han-a   (although I shall refuse)
      batu baba-ta-han-a   (people who will refuse)

(c) /-*ka*-/: affirmative potential, negative potential and negative future

e.g. *Ni-ka-zamay-a*   (I might go)
      Ne-ni-ka-zamay-a   (I might have gone)
      batu baba-ka-zamay-a   (people who might go)
      Ni-ka-si-zamay-i   (I shall not go)

alt. *Ni-ka-si-ke na zamay-a*
      Ne-ni-ka-si-zamay-i   (I would not have gone)

alt. *Ne-ni-si-ke na-zamay-a*
      batu baba-ka-si-tus-i   (people who will not/cannot help)

alt. *batu baba-si-ke ba-tus-a*

(d) /-*ka*-/: negative past

e.g. *A-ba-si-ka-tus-a*   (They did not help)
      niha ba-si-ka-ni-tus-a   (although they did not help me)
      batubaba-si-ka-ni-tus-a   (people who did not help me)

(e) /-*a*-/: affirmative subjunctive past

e.g. *Lufitile, lw-a-kal-a kuyaha* (We arrived and began to build)

(f) /**ku-**/: infinitive

e.g. ***ku**-fit-a*   (to arrive)

***ku**-sa-fit-a*   (not to arrive)

Aspect Signs

There are three morphemes which appear to be inflecting morphemes and which refine the inflection by implying continuing action.

(a) /**-sa-**/ (still; in the negative, no longer)

This morpheme occurs in affirmative primary inflections in the present, past and future. In the negative it appears to be restricted to the principal present inflexion.

e.g. *Ba-**sa**-lut-a*   (They still teach)

*A-lu-**sa**-zib-a*   (We no longer know)

(b) The form /**-sazo-**/ (just, recently) is restricted to the affirmative present.

e.g. *Ni-**sazo**-lek-a njinga*   (I have just bought a bicycle)

*niha ba-**sazo**-fit-a*   (although they have just arrived)

(c) /**-no-**/ (keep on, continue) is restricted to the negative imperative, the hortative, the present and past subjunctives, in which orders and requests are given. Some speakers restrict its use to the present subjunctive.

e.g. *Si-**no**-lif-i*   (Do not continue to pay)

*A-lu-**no**-itut-a*   (Let us keep on studying)

*Mu-**no**-itut-a*   (You must continue to study)

*Mu-si-**no**-ba-sebelez-a* (You must not go on working for

	them)
*Musike **mw-a-no**-sebez-a katata cwalo*	(You must not go on working as hard as that)

Terminals

Terminals are constituents of inflections which occur as suffixes to radicals in inflected VPs. They are thus discontinuous with the other inflecting morphemes with which they combine to form inflections. The forms and distribution are as follows:

(a) /-*i*/: negative present primary tenses, save when the aspect sign /-*sa*-/ is used,

e.g. ***Ha-ni**-lat-**i*** (I don't want)
cp. ***Ha-ni-sa**-lat-a* (I no longer want)
: negative imperative,
e.g. *si-zamay-**i**!* (do not go!)
*si-ba-bon-**i**!* (do not see them!)
: negative subjunctive, save when the aspect sign /-*no*-/ is used,
e.g. *I-**si**-ni-lum-**i*** (Let it not bite me!)
cp. *Lu-**si-no**-honon-a* (Let us not keep on doubting)
: affirmative "occasional" subjunctive
e.g. ***Ni-ti** ni-bulel-**i** siFura* (I sometimes speak French)

(b) /-*e*/: hortative and subjunctive present,
e.g. *Ha-lu-buz-**e*** (Let us ask)
*Ha-lu-y-**e**, lu-buz-**e*** (Let us go, and ask)
: imperative (i) affirmative and negative, with plural terminal;

(ii) affirmative, of a VP containing an object prefix;

(iii) after the auxiliary /-to-/.

e.g.	*Mat-e-ŋi!*	(Run! – plural)
	Si-lek-e-ŋi!	(Do not buy! – plural)
	Ba-bon-e!	(See them!)
	Si-ba-bon-e-ŋi!	(Do not see them! – plural)
	To-utw-e!	(Come and taste!)
alt.	*Ta **u**-utw-e!*	

(c) /-*ile*/: This is the terminal of the past tense of the primary inflections

e.g. *U-mu-bon-**ile*** (She saw him)

*Ba-fet-**ile*** (They have arrived)

This terminal is found in a number of other forms, viz.

- as /-*ize*/ after radicals ending in /c, j, s, sh, z, zw, ny/

e.g. -*bes-**ize*** (roasted)

- as /-*ine*/ after certain radicals ending in /n/

e.g. -*mumun-**ine*** (sucked)

- as /-*ite*/ after certain radicals ending in /t/

e.g. -*tubet-**ite*** (kissed)

- as /-*i*/ after radicals ending in /am/ and /an/

e.g. -*paham-**i*** (climbed)

-*kopan-**i*** (met)

- as /-*ezi*/ after radicals ending in /al/, /al/ being replaced by the terminal /-*ezi*/,

e.g. -*katez-**i*** (be tired)

cp. -*katal-* (get tired)

In many cases /-*ile*/ is a free alternant to the above,

e.g.   *-bonahezi ~ bonahalile*

cp.   *-bonahal-*   (be visible)

(d)   /-a/: Terminal /-a/ occurs in all other inflections.

THE BASIC CONJUGATION

The following is an outline of the inflections, each consisting of a combination of inflecting morphemes, which combine with VPs to form inflected VPs which are the predicates of verbal clauses. The inflections are divided according to the following categories.

1. finite and non-finite;
2. primary and secondary;
3. forms divided according to tense and aspect;
4. affirmative and negative.

Finite Inflections

(a) **Primary inflections**

    (i) PRESENT TENSE

       1. Affirmative

    - principal : long : subject prefix (sp) *-a-...-a*

e.g.   *W-a-lu-bon-a*   (He sees us)

           short: sp- ...-*a*

e.g.   *U-bon-a-ŋi?*   (What do you see?)

    The principal "long" inflection is used with VPs consisting of

         (a) a radical without complements or adjuncts;

         (b) an object prefix, a radical and object complements.

e.g.   ***Kw-a-fifal-a***   (It is getting dark)

         ***W-a-bu-lek-a**, bucwala*   (He is buying some beer)

The principal "short" inflection is used with VPs consisting of

    (a) a radical followed by the interrogative complements ***maɲi**?* (who?) and ***iɲi**? ~ -**ɲi**?* (what?)

    (b) a radical followed by an object or adverbial complement

e.g.   ***Ba**-ez-a-ɲi?*   (What are they doing?)

         ***Ba**-lek-a nama*   (They are buying meat)

         *Liiba **li**-fuf-a kamoya*   (The dove flies through the air)

- participial : sp-...-***a***

e.g.   *niha **ba**-lek-**a**..*   (although they buy meat..)

- relative : sp-...-***a***

e.g.   *batu **baba**-lek-a nama*   (people who buy meat)

2. Negative

- principal : **ha**-sp-...-*i*

e.g.   ***ha-ni**-lek-i nama*   (I don't buy meat)

- participial : sp-***sa***-...-*i*

e.g.   *haiba **mu-sa**-lek-i nama...*   (if you don't buy meat...)

- relative : sp-***sa***-...-*i*

e.g.   *batu **baba-sa**-lek-**i** nama*   (people who don't buy meat)

(ii) FUTURE TENSE
   1. Affirmative
   - principal : sp-***ta-***...-***a***
   e.g.   *Ni-**ta**-lek-a nama*   (I shall buy meat)

   - participial : sp-***ta-***...-***a***
   e.g.   *haiba **mu-ta**-zamay-a...*   (if you will go...)

   - relative : sp-***ta-***...-***a***
   e.g.   *batu **baba-ta**-lek-a nama*   (people who will buy meat)

   2. Negative (The potential tense is used)

(iii) POTENTIAL TENSE
   1. Affirmative
   - principal : sp-***ka-***...-***a***
   e.g.   *Ni-**ka**-lek-a nama*   (I might buy meat)

   - participial : sp-***ka-***...-***a***
   e.g.   *ne **ni-ka**-lek-a nama*   (I might have bought meat)

   - relative : sp-***ka-***...-***a***
   e.g.   *batu **baba-ka**-lek-a nama*   (people who may buy meat)

   2. Negative
   - principal : sp-***ka-si-***...-***i***
   e.g.   *Ni-**ka-si**-lek-i nama*   (I shall/may not buy meat)

- participipial : sp-***ka-si-***...-***i***

e.g.   *haiba bondate **ba-ka-si-lek-i** nama*   (if father will not/cannot buy meat...)

- relative : sp-***ka-si-***..***i***

e.g.   *batu **baba-ka-si-lek-i** nama*   (people who will not/cannot buy meat)

Some siLozi speakers prefer the use of an auxiliary verb construction here, the negative potential inflection of the auxiliary verb phrase: /-*ke*/ followed by a past subjunctive.

e.g.   ***Ni-ka-si-ke** naleka nama*   (I shall not buy meat)

*Nihaiba bondate **ba-si-ke** baleka nama...*   (Although my father will not buy meat...)

*Batu **baba-si-ke** baleka nama...*   (People who will not buy meat...)

(iv) PAST TENSE

    1. Affirmative

    - principal : sp-...-***ile***

e.g.   ***Ni-lek-ile** nama*   (I have bought meat)

    - participipial : sp-...-***ile***

e.g.   *Nihaiba **ba-lek-ile** nama...*   (If they have bought meat...)

    - relative : sp-...-***ile***

e.g.   *Batu **baba-lek-ile** nama*   (People who have bought meat)

2. Negative

- principal : **ha**-sp-*si-ka*-...-*a*

e.g.   ***Ha-ni-si-ka**-lek-a nama*   (I have not bought meat)

- participial : sp-*si-ka*-...-*a*

e.g.   *Nihaiba **mu-si-ka**-ni-tus-a...*   (Although you did not help me...)

- relative : sp-*si-ka*-...-*a*

e.g.   *Batu **baba-si-ka**-ni-tus-a...*   (People who did not help me...)

(v) PROGRESSIVE ASPECT

1. Affirmative

- principal present : sp-*sa*-...-*a*

e.g.   ***Ni-sa**-lut-a*   (I still teach)

- principal future : sp-*sa-ta*-...-*a*

e.g.   ***Ba-sa-ta**-lek-a nama*   (They will still buy meat)

Some Lozi prefer the auxiliary verb construction

e.g.   ***Ba-ta**-be **ba-sa**-lek-a nama*   (They will be still buying meat)

- principal past (of VPs with inchoative radicals[1]) sp-*sa*...-*ile*

e.g.   ***Ba-sa**-lap-**ile***   (They are still hungry)

Participial and relative forms of the above inflections exist.

---

[1] i.e. radicals which signify states or conditions that come into being, e.g. *-lap-* (become hungry).

2. Negative
- principal present : ha-sp-*sa*...*a*

e.g.   *Ha-ni-sa-zub-a*   (I no longer smoke)

This is the only negative inflection containing /-sa-/ which has been noted.

(b) Secondary inflections

(i) HORTATIVE

1. Affirmative : **ha**-sp-...-*e*

e.g.   *Ha-lu-y-e-ŋi*   (Let us all go)

2. Negative : **ha**-sp-*si*-...-*i*

e.g.   *Ha-lu-si-zw-i*   (Let us not go out)

Some siLozi speakers use the negative subjunctive of the appropriate auxiliary verb phrase here.

e.g.   *Lu-si-ke lw-a-zw-a*   (We must not go out)

(ii) "PRESENT" SUBJUNCTIVE

1. Affirmative : sp-...-*e*

e.g.   *kuli **ni**-lek-e nama*   (that I may buy meat)

2. Negative : sp-*si*-...-*i*

e.g.   *kuli **ni-si**-lek-i nama*   (that I may not buy meat)

or   *kuli **ni-si-ke** naleka nama*   (so that I may not buy meat)

Some siLozi speakers use the negative sign /-sa/ here

*kuli **ni-sa**-lek-i nama*   (so that I don't buy meat)

(iii) "PAST" SUBJUNCTIVE

    1. Affirmative sp-*a*-...-*a*

e.g.   *mane **b**-**a**-lobal-**a***   (until they slept)

(iv) "OCCASIONAL" SUBJUNCTIVE

This is the term used by Gowlett for the inflection of VPs occurring as complements after the auxiliary radicals /-*ne*/ and /-*ti* ~ -*te*/ as indicating occasional action. Only the affirmative is given: Sp-......-*i*

e.g.   *I-**ne** i-nel-**i***   (It sometimes rains)

As Gowlett states, this inflection is not recognised by many speakers.

(v) THE "CONTINUOUS" ASPECT

    1. Affirmative

    - hortative : ***ha***-sp-***no***-...-*a*

e.g.   ***Ha-lu-no**-ikut-**a***   (Let us keep on studying)

    - "present" subjunctive : sp-***no***-...-*a*

e.g.   ***Lu-no**-itut-**a***   (We must keep on studying)
    Mu-no**-itut-**a   (You must keep on studying)

    - "past" subjunctive as complement of the Auxiliary Radical /-*ke*/: sp-***a-no***-...-*a*

e.g.   *Basike **b-a-no**-nw-**a** kofi ahulu*   (They ought not to continue drinking so much coffee)

    2. Negative

    - imperative : *si-no-...-i*

e.g.   *Si-no-lek-i*   (Don't continue to buy)

- "present" subjunctive : sp-*si-no-*...-*a*

e.g.   *mu-si-no*-ba-sebelez-*a*   (you should not keep on working for them)

NON-FINITE INFLECTIONS

(a) **The infinitive**

   1. Affirmative : *ku-*...-*a*

e.g.   *ku-lek-a nama*   (to buy meat)

   2. Negative : *ku-sa-*...-*a*

e.g.   *ku-sa-lek-a nama*   (not to buy meat)

(b) **The imperative**

   1. Affirmative :

      - singular : ...-*a*

e.g.   *lek-a nama!*   (buy meat!)

      - plural : ...-*e-ŋi* ~ -*a-ŋi*

e.g.   *lek-e-ŋi nama!*   (buy meat! – plural)

VPs containing an object prefix have the following inflections:

      : ...-*e*, ...-*e-ŋi*

e.g.   *i-lek-e!*   (buy it!)

    i-lek-e-ŋi!   (buy it! – plural)

2. Negative

- singular : **si-...-i**

e.g. **si-lek-i!**   (do not buy!)

- plural : **si-...-e-ŋi**

e.g. **si-lek-e-ŋi!**   (do not buy! – plural)

VPs containing an object prefix have the following inflections

: ...-i, ...-e-ŋi

e.g. **si-i-lek-i!**   (do not buy it!)

si-i-lek-e-ŋi!   (do not buy it! – plural)

Some siLozi speakers prefer to use the negative subjunctive with negative sign /-sa-/ for prohibitions.

e.g. **u-sa-lek-i!**   (do not buy!)

AUXILIARY VERB CONSTRUCTIONS

Inflected VPs are the simplest type of verbal construction which belongs to the constituent class of predicate. A more complicated verbal construction consists of the inflected auxiliary verb phrase. In this latter construction the two constituents are (1) the inflection and (2) the auxiliary verb phrase. For example, in the inflected auxiliary VP,

ku-to-utwa bucwala   (to come and taste beer)

the auxiliary VP consists of the auxiliary radical /-to-/ (come and) followed by its complement, /-utw-a bucwala/, an /...-a/ inflected VP, viz. /-to-utwa bucwala/.

The inflection of the auxiliary VP consists of the infinitive prefix /ku-/

e.g.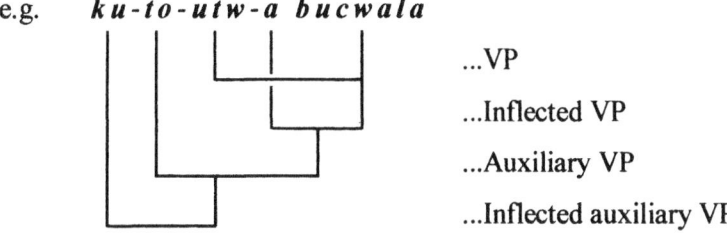
...VP
...Inflected VP
...Auxiliary VP
...Inflected auxiliary VP

In the inflected auxiliary VP,

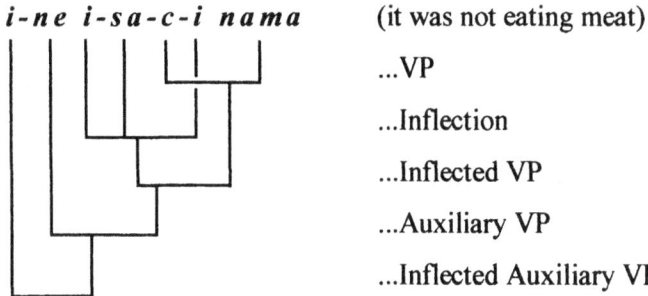 (it was not eating meat)
...VP
...Inflection
...Inflected VP
...Auxiliary VP
...Inflected Auxiliary VP

the auxiliary VP consists of the auxiliary radical /-ne/ (was) followed by its complement /i-sa-c-i nama/, (it not eating meat), a negative participial present inflected VP.

The Auxiliary Verb

There are a number of auxiliary verbs in siLozi. They differ from ordinary verbs in that the complements which they require are not objects and adjuncts but, instead, verb phrases, the verbal constructions of Level 2. Compare the two types of constructional pattern involved. The constructional pattern of the verb phrase is:

/+/- object prefix + verb radical +/- complement(s) +/- adjunct(s).

e.g. /-utw- bucwala/ (taste beer) : /-c-nama/ (eat meat)

That of the auxiliary verb phrase is:

/+ auxiliary verb + verb phrase/

e.g. /-to -utw- bucwala/ (come and taste beer) : /-ne -c- nama/ (was eating meat)

The verb phrases, e.g. /-**utw- bucwala**/ and /-**c- nama**/, both illustrated in the diagrams and in the examples above, become complements by being variously inflected according to the requirements of the type of auxiliary verb. For example, the auxiliary verb /-**to**/ requires a contracted infinitive VP (i.e. an infinitive VP without its prefix /**ku-**/ and which is inflected merely by the terminal vowel /-**a**/.) Hence the complement is /-**utw-a bucwala**/. The auxiliary verb /-**ne**/ requires a participially inflected VP which is inflected by a subject prefix, other inflecting morphemes according to tense, aspect, etc., and a terminal vowel. In our example the complement is /**i-sa-c-i nama**/ in which the inflection is /sp: **i**-, negative infix: -**sa**- and the terminal vowel: -**i**/.

Just as ordinary verb phrases need an inflection, not only of the complementary verb phrase, but also of the auxiliary with its inflected complement, as an accompanying constituent to the verb phrase in order to form a predicate, so auxiliary verb phrases also need an inflection to become a predicate. In the case of the predicate: /**ku-toutwa bucwala**/ the inflection is just the infinitive prefix /**ku-**/. But in the case of the predicate /**i-ne i-sici nama**/, which exemplifies the auxiliary verb /-**ne**/, the inflection has to be one which applies to both auxiliary verb and complementary verb phrase. The complement has not only to be participially inflected but shown as having the same subject prefix as the auxiliary verb as both parts of the inflected auxiliary verb construction refer to the same subject.

Another example: Auxiliary VP: /-na -pil- hamunati nibana bahae/

(was living pleasantly with his children)

Inflected auxiliary VP: /U-na a-pil- hamunati nibana bahae/
(He was living pleasantly with his children)

The following are some of the types of auxiliary radical, differentiated according to the nature of the complement they control.

(a) Auxiliary verb followed by an /...-a/ inflected VP (perhaps a contracted infinitive VP),[1]

viz.
(i) /-to-/ (come and) cp. /-t-/ (come)
(ii) /-tilo-/ (have come and)
(iii) /-yo-/ (go and) cp. /-y-/ (go)
(iv) /-ilo-/ (have gone to, gone and)
(v) /-mano-/ (do as soon as) cp. /-man-/ (finish)
(vi) -sino-/ (do as soon as)
(vii) /-zo-/ (after) cp. /-zw-/ (come from)

e.g.
(i) *Lila li-**to**-lulwanisa*[2] (The enemy is coming to attack us)
*Ha-a-**to**-lubona* (She is not coming to see us)
*Mu-**to**-bona* (You must come and see us)
(v) *A-**mano**-fita, lwamulumelisa* (As soon as he had arrived, we greeted him)
(vi) *Ni-**sino**-zamaya, likomu zazwa* (No sooner do I leave than the cattle go out)

[1.] The auxiliary radicals in this section are treated as verb stems. It is believed that their terminal vowel /-o/ is the result of a contraction between a former terminal vowel /-a/ and the infinitive prefix /ku-/ of complements, /-a + ku-/ > /-o-/.
[2.] In this section the auxiliary verb phrases are in bold in examples.

(vii) *U-sa-zo-fita*   (He has just arrived)

The inflection of auxiliary VPs with the above auxiliary radicals is not uniform. It is stated in great detail in Gowlett, *The Special Conjugational Series.* (1967)

(b) Auxiliary radical followed by an infinitive inflected VP,

viz.
- (i)   /-*atis*-/   (do often;   as non-auxiliary – increase)
- (ii) /-*bat*-/   (do nearly;   – seek, want)
- (iii) /-*buel*-/   (do again;   – return)
- (iv) /-*ekez*-/   (do again;   – augment)
- (v)   /-*pakis*-/ (do quickly;   – hurry)
- (vi) /-*swal*-/   (keep on doing;   – seize)

Of these auxiliary radicals all but /-*atis*-/, and sometimes it as well, are followed by affirmative participial present complements as alternatives, with meaning equivalent to the infinitive complements.

e.g.
- (i)   *Ni-atis-a kutaha kwanu*   (I often come here)
- (ii) *Ne-lu-bat-ile kushwa*   (We nearly died)
        Ne-ba-bat-ile bawela mwanuka   (They nearly fell into the river)
- (iii) *Ni-ka-buel-a nikula*   (I may fall sick again)
        Mutu u-buezi kuyema   (The person got up again)
- (iv) *Ne-ba-ekez-a kubulela*   (They spoke again)
        Ne-ba-ekez-a babulela   (They spoke again)
- (v)   *U-pakis-ize kuiesa*   (He did it quickly)
        U-pakis-ize aieza   (He did it quickly)
        Ni-ta-pakis-a niieza   (I shall do it soon)

	(vi)	*Bashimani ba-sweli kukanana*	(The boys keep on discussing)
		Bashimani ba-sweli bakanana	(The boys keep on discussing)

(c) Auxiliary verbs followed by participial inflected VPs of all tenses,

viz. (i)   /-ba/   (be)
    (ii) /-ne/   (be)
    (iii) /-se/   (do now, do already)

(i) Auxiliary VPs with /-ne/ as auxiliary verb are inflected only to the extent of prefixing of vowel subject prefixes: to the auxiliary /-ne/ plus, of course, the full participial inflection of the complementary VP. The tense is past.

e.g.
	Ne-nizamaya	(I was walking)
	Ne-nisazamayi	(I was not walking)
	Ne-nizamayile	(I had walked)
	Ne-nisikazamaya	(I had not walked)
	Ne-nitazamaya	(I was about to walk)
	Ne-nikasike nazamaya	(I was not about to walk)

(ii) Auxiliary verb /-se/ is followed only by affirmative participial complements. It is not normally inflected save when it is itself part of a participial complement following /-ne/.

e.g.
	Se-nizamaya	(Now I am walking)
	Se-lusilile **mabele**	(We have already ground the corn)
	Se-lutafita	(We will soon arrive)
	Ne-ni-**se** nizamaya	(I was already walking)

*Ba-se batile **kwanu***	(They have already come here)
*Ne-ni-se ni**baboni***	(I had already seen them)
*Nise niya **kumulena***	(I am now going to the chief)

(iii) Auxiliary VPs with /-ba ~ -be/ are inflected in the future

e.g.
*Ni-ta-**be** ni**z**amaya*	(I shall be walking)
*Ni-ta-**be** ni**z**amayile*	(I shall have walked) etc.

(d) Auxiliary radicals and verbs followed by present participial inflected VPs,

viz. (i) /-*fitel*-/ (until; as non-auxiliary – arrive at)

e.g. *Ululibelezi ku-**fitel**-a lufita* (He waited for us until we should arrive)

(ii) /-*kut*-/ (again; as non-auxiliary – return)

e.g. *Nita-**kut**-a nimubona* (I shall see you again)

(iii) /-*li*/ (while; as non-auxiliary – say, do)

e.g.
*A-**li** asabulela, kwataha mwan'ahae*	(While he was still speaking, his child came)
*Ni-**li** nisa**bahupula**, nise nibabona bafita*	(While I was still thinking of them, I saw them coming)
*Ba-**li** bahoha **mukolo**, baupalelwa*	(They were pushing the canoe and it was too much for them)
*Ni-sa-**li** niba **mutu**, hanisikasieza*	(Ever since I became a man, I have not done this)
*Ni-sa-**li** ni**ke**na **mwandu**, hanisikamubona*	(Ever since I came into the house, I have not seen him)

U-ta-li ufita kwakota yani, (You will arrive, or, when you arrive,
utabona nuka at that tree, you will see the river)

   (iv)   /*-na*/   (keep on doing)

   (v)   /*-nze*/   (continue)

e.g.   *Ni-nze nisebeza*   (I go on working)
      Ne-ni-nze nisebeza   (I went on working)
      U-nzo umuluta?   (Do you still teach him?)
      U-sa-nze azamaya   (He is still walking)

   (vi)   /*-swan-*/   (perhaps; as non-auxiliary – be like)
      Pizi ika-swan-a isaba   (The horse may run away)

   (vii)   /*-tol-*/ (neg)   (not again; as non-auxiliary – spend the day)
      Ha-ni-sa-tol-a nieza hape   (I shall never more do it again)
      Ha-ni-tol-i nieza   (I never do it any more)

   (viii)   /*-tuh-*/   (soon, probably; as non-auxiliary – start)
      Kifakaufi, ni-ta-tuh-a niyofita   (It is near, I shall soon arrive)
      U-ta-tuh-a atolupotela   (He will soon visit us)

(e) Auxiliary verbs followed by present subjunctive inflected VPs.

viz.   (i)   /*-be*/   (until)
     (ii)   /*-ke*/   (potentiality)
     (iii) /*-li*/   (intention)
     (iv) /*-te*/   (until)

(v) /-buel-/ (again)

(i) Auxiliary VPs with /-be/ as auxiliary verb are normally inflected in the present subjunctive

e.g. *Lutasebeza a-**be** afite* (We shall work until he arrives)

(ii) VPs as complements to /-ke/ as auxiliary verb are normally inflected in the affirmative perfect

e.g. *Ni-**ke** nieze* (I could do it)
*Ne-ni-**ke** nieze* (I could have done it)

(iii) Auxiliary VPs with /-li/ as auxiliary are widely inflected and require a complementary VP in the present subjunctive inflection. The auxiliary VP conveys action aimed at or attempted.

e.g. *Nizamaya ku-li nifite* (I walk in order that I may arrive)
Ne-nizamaya ku-li nifite (I was walking in order that I might arrive)
Ne-ni-li nisile kono napalelwa (I was intending to cross but I was unable)
*Ne-ba-li bahohe **mukolo** kono baupalelwa* (They were endeavouring to move the canoe but they were unable)
Lumulibelezi ku-li ate (We waited for him to come)

(iv) Auxiliary VPs with /-t-/ as auxiliary radical are inflected in the present subjunctive to form a future subjunctive of the auxiliary VP.

e.g. *Ba-sebez-ile kuli ba-**t**-e bazamaye kwahae* (They worked until they eventually went home)

| | *Zamaya uyomubulela kuli* | (Go and tell him that he should go to |
| | *a-t-e alobale* | sleep) |

    (v) /*-buel-*/
e.g.   *Nita-**buel**-a niifose*   (I will get it wrong again)

(f) Auxiliary radical followed by past subjunctive inflected VPs,

viz.   (i) /*-ke*/   (negative potentiality)
    (ii) /*-li*/   (intention)
    (iii) /*-swan-*/   (possibility; as non-auxiliary - resemble)

    (i) Auxiliary VPs with /*-ke*/ as auxiliary radical are inflected in the negative principal potential and participial future, as well as in the negative subjunctive.

e.g.   *Ha-ni-ka-**ke** naieza*   (I could not have done it)
    *Ni-ka-si-**ke** nahalifa*   (I will not, would/ not get angry)
    *Niha ba-si-**ke** bahalifa..*   (Although they will not get angry..)
    *Ne-ba-si-**ke** bahalifa..*   (They would not have got angry)
    *..kuli ni-si-**ke** naziba*   (..so that I might not know)

    (ii) Auxiliary VPs with /*-li*/ as auxiliary radical are inflected in the present.

e.g.   *Ni-**li** nazamaya*   (I am about to go, intending to go)
    *Ne-ni-**li** nazamaya*   (I was on the point of going)

    (iii) Auxiliary VPs with /*-swan-*/ are inflected in the potential.

e.g.   *Lu-ka-**swan**-a lwamubona*   (We are likely to see him)

A-ka-swan-a alubona (He is likely to see us)

(g) Auxiliary radical followed by "occasional" subjunctive inflected VPs,

viz.   (i) /-ne/   (sometimes, occasionally)

     (ii) /-ti ~ -te/   (occasionally)

Auxiliary VPs with /-ne/ and /-ti ~ -te/ as auxiliary radicals are inflected in the present.

e.g.   (i) *I-ne ineli*   (It occasionally rains)

      Nja ine ilumi bapoti   (The dog sometimes bites visitors)

     (ii) *Ni-ti nibuleli siFura*   (I sometimes speak French)

These constructions do not seem to be generally recognised.

THE VERBAL CLAUSE AND SENTENCE

The clause as a construction consists of a subject and a predicate. The constituent of subject is optional but that of predicate is compulsory. In verbal clauses the predicate is either an inflected VP or an inflected auxiliary VP.

There are as many types of clause as there are major types of inflection. Thus there are principal, participial, relative, hortative, subjunctive, infinitive and imperative clauses differing from each other in inflection.

Sentences, the units of utterance, are made up of combinations of clauses. Statements and questions normally contain principal clauses as their nucleus and this nucleus is often extended by participial or subjunctive clauses. Hortative and imperative sentences contain clauses with these inflections as their nucleus and they are often extended by subjunctive clauses.

Sentences may consist of principal clauses joined by the conjunctives /*mi*/ (and then), /*kona*/ (but), /*fela*/ (but), /*kapa*/ (or) and others.

e.g. **Ufelize musebezi wahae mwamasimu *mi* ukutezi kwahae**   (He finished his work in the fields and went home)

Niutwile *kono* haniutwisisi   (I have heard but I do not understand)

Neniboni tapi *fela* nenisikaiswala   (I saw the fish but I did not catch it)

Lukayaha ndu *kapa* lukayolima?   (Are we to build the house or go to till the land?)

Haasebezi kuzwafo haakoni kufepa lubasi lwahae   (He does not work and therefore cannot support his family)

Sentences may consist of combinations of principal or imperative clauses and participial clauses. The latter are often introduced and linked to the principal clauses by conjunctives such as the following: /*ha-*/ (if, when), /*haiba*/ (if), /*niha*/ (although), /*nihaiba*/ (although), /*pili*/ (while), /*kaha*/ (because).

e.g. **Ha nisazibi, nitakubulelela cwaŋi?**   (If I do not know how can I tell you?)

Kaha mulikani anitusize, nitakutusa niwena   (Because your friend helped me, I shall help you also)

Pili asazamaya, ubonani niyena   (While she was still walking, she met him)

Niha kuli cwalo, usakona kusebeza musebezi wahae   (Although that is the case, he is still able to do his work)

Usike waeza lilata, ha   (Do not make a noise while he is *asabulela* speaking)

Sentences may consist of combinations of principal or imperative clauses and subjunctive clauses. These combinations often convey consecutive action. Present subjunctive inflection follows present tense signs. Past subjunctive inflection generally follows past and potential forms[1].

e.g. *Itute, utalife ha usali yomunca* (Study and be educated while you are still young)

Utaluŋolela (He will write to us and inform us
aluzibise bupilo bwabahesu about our relatives' health)
Utaluŋolela liŋolo (He will write letters to us and we
lute lutabe kuliamuhela will be glad to get them)
Nikakumatisa nikuswale (I can chase and catch you)
Haiba noha ilubona, (If the snake sees us, it could swim to
ikatapela kwanu, yaluluma us and bite us)
Wasebeza (He works until he finishes his work)
mane afeze musebezi wahae
Una asebeza (He worked until he finished his work)
mane afeza musebezi wahae
Niyemele mane nite nikute (Wait for me until I return)
Una aniyemezi mane nakuta (He waited for me until I returned)
Folofolo iboni tau (The buck saw the lion and then ran
cwale yasaba away)

---

[1] Each clause is underlined to show the different clauses making up the sentence. Where a sentence takes up two lines a new clause begins on the second line.

Chapter 3
IDEOPHONIC CONSTRUCTIONS

Not many siLozi ideophones have been recorded nor do the constructions in which ideophones occur as constituents figure in the literature. The following are some random examples of ideophones, in some cases reduplicated.

cupwi, ngumbwi, tupwi	(falling into water)
culu	(going away for good)
cupwa cupwa	(walking in water)
cwaa	(being sour, of liquids)
mbilu	(paddling fast)
nga nga nga	(shivering)
ngaa	(biting)
ngo, tuu, twi	(keeping quiet)
nyame nyame	(disappearing)
pululu	(being grey in colour)
temu temu	(looking round speechless)
twaa	(being bright)
wi	(being dark)
wulukutu	(falling down)
yaku	(seizing)
yubu	(splashing of water)

It appears that ideophonic phrases analogous to inflected verb phrases but very different from them in style are constructed according to the following pattern:

ideophone +/- complement(s) +/- adjunct(s)

e.g.   *culu kwabukuwa*   (going off for good to the white man's country)

       tupwi mwanuka   (falling into the river)

Ideophonic phrases are normally found as constituents of auxiliary verb phrases with radical /-li/. These auxiliary VPs are inflected and form the predicates of clauses.

e.g.   *Licwe neli-**li tupwi mwanuka***[1]   (The stone fell into the river)

       *Naaile a-**li culu kwabukuwa***   (He had gone off for good to the white man's country)

       *Bazamaya mwamezi ba-**li cupwa cupwa***   (They are walking in the water, splashing along)

       *Mabisi a-**li cwaa***   (The milk is sour)

       *Ukuzize a-**li tuu***   (He kept quiet)

       *Kuza u-**li ngo!***   (Keep quiet!)

       *Naakeni mwandu akuza a-**li twi***   (He came into the room and kept quite quiet)

       *Naakeni mwandu. Kiha ase aina, a-**li twi***   (He came into the house. That is when he sat down quietly)

       *Naamulumile a-**li ngaa***   (He bit him)

       *Folofolo neimata i-**li nyame nyame***   (The buck ran away, disappearing into the distance)

       *Naawile a-**li wulukutu inge kota***   (He fell down heavily like a tree)

       *Naafuluha mukolo a-**li mbilu***   (He was paddling the canoe strongly)

       *Mukolo noumata u-**li mbilu***   (The canoe was going very fast)

       *Lizazi li-**li twaa***   (The sun is bright)

---

[1] The auxiliary verb phrases consisting of /-li/ and ideophonic phrases as complements are in bold in examples in this section.

*Busihu bu-**li wi***	(The night is dark)
*Mezi a-**li yubu mwapiza***	(The water is splashing out of the pot)
*Nja neikeni mwandu, yafita fanama, ya-**li yaku kameno***	(The dog entered the house, drew near to the meat, and seized it with his teeth)

Ideophonic phrases may, however, function as predicates in ideophonic clauses.

e.g. *Mwan'aka culu kwabukuwa* (My child went off for good to the white man's country)

BIBLIOGRAPHY

Fortune, G. "A Note on the Languages of Barotseland" in *The History of the Central African Peoples*. Paper presented at the Seventeenth Conference of the Rhodes-Livingstone Institute for Social Research, Lusaka 1963, pp. 26 and map.

Fortune, G. "The Languages of the Western Province of Zambia", *Journal of the Language Association of Eastern Africa*, Vol. 1, No. 1, pp. 31-39, and map.

Gorman, W.A.R. *Simple Silozi*, Longmans, London 1950.

Gowlett, D.F. *Morphology of the Substantive in Lozi*, B.A. Honours Dissertation, Department of African Languages, University of the Witwatersrand, 1964.

Gowlett, D.F. *Morphology of the Verb in Lozi*, M.A. Dissertation, Department of African Languages, University of the Witwatersrand, 1967.

Gowlett, D.F. 1989. "The Parentage and Development of Lozi" in *Journal of African Languages and Linguistics*, Vol. 11, No. 2, pp. 127-149.

Jalla, A. *Dictionary of the Lozi Language*, Vol. 1, Lozi-English, U.S.C.L. London 1936.

Jalla, A. *Elementary Grammar of the Lozi Language*, U.S.C.L. London 1937.

Kashoki, M.E. 1981. "Harmonisation of African Languages: Standardisation of Orthography in Zambia" in *African Languages: Proceedings of the Meeting of Experts on the Transcription and Harmonisation of African Languages*. Paris: UNESCO, pp. 164-175.

Kay, G. *A Social Geography of Zambia*, University of London Press, 1967.

Lewanika, G.A.M. *English-Lozi Phrase Book*, Macmillan, London, 1956.

Yukawa, Y. 1987. "A Tonological Study of Lozi Verbs" in *Bantu Linguistics (IILCAA) (Studies in Zambian Languages)*, Vol. 1, pp. 73-128.

www.ingramcontent.com/pod-product-compliance
Lightning Source LLC
Chambersburg PA
CBHW061959220426
43662CB00011B/1743